NAALADIYAR

NAALADIYAR

PALANI. ARANGASAMY

Published by
Rupa Publications India Pvt. Ltd 2022
7/16, Ansari Road, Daryaganj
New Delhi 110002

Sales centres:
Allahabad Bengaluru Chennai
Hyderabad Jaipur Kathmandu
Kolkata Mumbai

Copyright © Palani Arangasamy 2022

The views and opinions expressed in this book are the author's own and the facts are as reported by him which have been verified to the extent possible, and the publishers are not in any way liable for the same.

All rights reserved.
No part of this publication may be reproduced, transmitted, or stored in a retrieval system, in any form or by any means, electronic, mechanical, photocopying, recording or otherwise, without the prior permission of the publisher.

ISBN: 978-93-5520-588-9

First impression 2022

10 9 8 7 6 5 4 3 2 1

The moral right of the author has been asserted.

Printed in India

This book is sold subject to the condition that it shall not, by way of trade or otherwise, be lent, resold, hired out, or otherwise circulated, without the publisher's prior consent, in any form of binding or cover other than that in which it is published.

NAALADIYAAR

(In English Version with Commentary)

FOREWORD

Dr. S. Thangamuthu,
Former Principal,
Rajah's College, Thiruvaiyaru.

Translation is an art that unifies the whole world into an intellectual repository. In a multi-lingual country of ours, its use is immense. The resultant effect of translation is unity in diversity. Its origin goes back to the period of written literature in developed languages. The *Tolkappiam*, an earliest extant of Tamil grammatical treatise makes a reference to translation. So the art of translation is as old as the age of written literature in Tamil.

Nowadays, it is taught as an academic discipline. It is variously known as transcreation, transmutation and transmogrification. Adaptation and synoptic rendering are also inclusive of this category. The present English rendering of *Naaladiyaar* may very well be termed as a faithful translation.

Prof. Arangasamy is eminently qualified to do this job. Having studied Tamil language and literature for four years exclusively in an Oriental College, he undertook the study of English Literature and did his doctorate in the analytical study of the Tamil translations of Shakespeare plays. Receipient of state award for Translation in 2019. His publishers include the Macmillan, Blackie, The Sahitya Academy, Emerald, National Book Trust (NBT) and Tamil University.

Besides being a bi-lingual scholar, he is an eloquent speaker, writer, poet, editor and a veteran translator. The English version of *Naaladiyaar* has got a critical comment under each one of the poems. Ideas that are identical to those of Tamil and English treatises are pointed out, wherever possible. Substance of certain quatrains are critically viewed to be in consonance with those of modern readers. Metrical sequences, rhetorical flourishes and various figures of speech such as onomatopoeia and allusions are also pointed out.

Some of the precepts are strongly and threateningly conveyed in *Naaladiyaar*. In preaching to avoid the habit of killing and eating aquatic reptiles such as crabs and fishes, the poet warns that if one eats crabs by breaking their legs, he would become leprotic in the next birth. Non-violence and vegetarianism are thus very strongly insisted here.

It is my personal view that many of the translated poems of *Naaladiyar* are more easily understandable than the original Tamil poems that are obscure with words out-dated, precise and abstract.

Similar translation of various other ethical treatises, the translator may undertake in the days to come for the benefit of scholarly public.

INTRODUCTION

Naaladi Nanooru

This anthology of four hundred quatrains is as well-known as *Tirukkural*, an outstanding earlier ethical treatise of Tamil, roughly of the 2nd century A.D. The *Naaladiyaar* is said to have been composed by a large number of Jain monks proficient in Tamil and Sanskrit. For a very long time, it was customary to prescribe for study a few poems from *Naaladiyaar* in the Tamil textbooks of secondary schools. This desirable academic practice may be continued for instilling confidence, discipline and intellectuality among the young.

Legend has it that a large number of Jain monks were patronised by a ruler of Pandiya country probably in the 9th Cent A.D. When they all wanted to go back to their own country, the ruler was unwilling to bid farewell to them. So inspired he was with the company of those great saintly-poets. But the monks have nocturnally left, leaving behind in the royal court, a quatrain each under their seats. The enraged king ordered the scripts to be thrown into the river, Vaigai. Surprisingly a good number of scripts, resisted the swift current of the river and came ashore. On scrutiny, each one was containing a precept essential for mankind. The king ordered them to be collected.

It is this collection, the king named *Naaladiyaar* and got it published. Perhaps because of the fact that it is said to have been written by individual poets, no single system of philosophy or theme can be deduced from them excepting the fact that the poems are suggestive of benevolent principles and moral purport. Even if the story is deemed to be apocryphal, nobody can gainsay that the authorship goes to a group of Jain ascetics, who in a number of poems highlight the importance of charity, truth and renunciation. It has to be added that on the whole, these epigrammatic stanzas are ethical, philosophical and didactic.

Reference to any god or religion is nil in the whole lot of poems, even though the authors are said to be the Jain monks. But a belief in re-birth and references to Heaven and Hell are found in them . Attainment of Heavenly bliss, known as *Mukthi* is hinted at. Morality, charity and righteousness are emphasised. Avoidance of anger and advocacy of renunciation are highlighted. The role of destiny is frequently marked out for its importance.

Both in style and thematic content, *Tirukkural* and *Naaladiyar* are almost alike. A set of 30 quatrains at the fag end of this treatise is devoted to lust and love. The ten poems at the outset from 371 to 380 condemn the volatality and mercurial temperament of harlots and counsels us to avoid those professionals. Another ten poems that succeed delineate the virtuous qualities of housewife such as patience, domesticity and genuine love and above all, a toleration of her husband even when he goes astray. She is pictured as an embodiment of morality and fobearance. Not known why the morality of men is not insisted with equal vehemance and their immorality is not condemned. Neo-classic feminists may criticise this partiality. The rest of the poems at the end speaks about the feigned anger of the lady on the one hand and her boldness in accompanying him to go on elopement.

Verbal juggleries such as puns and equivocations are almost nil except in one or two places - such as puns in 39 and 56. In poems 4 and 25, onomatopoeia defies translation. Except occasional literary echoes of *Tirukkural*, explicit references or indebtedness to early poems are very rare to be found. This ensures the originality of thinking among the monks. They drew inspiration from what they saw in Nature. Ideas extraordinary were born to them from things ordinary. That was the unique talent among the versatile poets.

One Tamil poet Pathumanar is said to be the earliest to edit and comment on the collection of these didactic poems. He has added an invocation also. Ever since, a number of editions and commentaries have come out to illuminate the essence of this ethical treatise. But the present edition has carefully followed a voluminous commentary of Chembur Vidwan V. Arumugam Servai. He had the favour of getting it serialised in a Tamil journal presently extinct *Ananda bodhini*. It cannot but be said that popular Tamil journals were particular in providing adequate coverage for language and literature unlike the modern periodicals that are vying with one another in giving excessive importance to cinematic news, advertisements, sports and games.

Adequate leisure that I enjoyed during my visiting professorship in the Dept. of Indology in Cologne University, Germany in 2015 enabled me to draft the first version. It was given one or two revisions subsequently with the guidance of the Tamil commentary of veteran scholar Arumugam Servai before finalising the script.

Every poem, wherever possible is followed by critical comments which in some respects are identifiable to the views of modernists. Poems and ideas that are comparable to that of other poets are also pointed out. My bilingual scholarship kept me in good stead to do the translation by myself and I daresay that I haven't consulted any earlier edition, either Tamil or English rendition excepting the one by Chembur Arumugam Servai. This may kindly be not misconstrued for my audacity. Just a confidence to stand on my own legs.

Discriminating readers are at liberty to point out blemishes, if any and I will have them corrected and incorporated in the next reprint. Mr. R. Subbarayalu, eminent writer and my friend encouraged me in this venture. I cannot but gratefully acknowledge his well-wishes. I thank immensely for Prof. S. Thangamuthu's Scholarly comments and critical remarks made at the time of working on this translation.

I acknowledge with thanks the typing and printing work of my young friend Mr. K.V. Karunanithi. But for him, this work would not have seen the light of day.

Thanjavur-613 004.   **Palani. Arangasamy**
03.01.2020

NAALADIYAAR

Invocation

Unaware we are even the origin of bow on the sky
Let's pray God, whose feet doesn't touch the ground
By bowing our head so low as to put it on the earth
To fulfil what all good that we earnestly thought of.

Blissful ignorance of ours is how and when the richly hued rainbow will appear on the bluish sky. With such unawareness, we humbly bow our head to God that he may be pleased to bestow on us what all we expect to succeed.

வான் இடு வில்லின் வரவறியா வாய்மையால்
கால்நிலம் தோயாக் கடவுளை-யாம் நிலம்
சென்னியுற வணங்கிச் சேர்தும் எம் உள்ளத்து
முன்னியவை முடிக என்று.

This Invocation is by Pathumanar, a poet of later ages

Division - 1

Chapter 1 - Instability of wealth
***

1. Even fabulous rich fed by husifs the wholesome food
   Of six varieties and reject the second course may even
   Descend to beg, shows wealth in the world
   Is not of perennial value.

   Customary it is in rich homes that young wives would feed their loving husbands endearingly. Surfeit of food is such that they would not take anything more even from their endearing wives. Even those fabulous rich may even come down to straightened circumstances in life is an indication that wealth is not constant. Six variety in culinary art includes Sweet, Sour, Pungency, Bitterness, Salty and Astringency. Husif-housewife.

   > அறு சுவை உண்டி அமர்ந்து இல்லாள் ஊட்ட
   > மறு சிகை நீக்கி உண்டாரும், வறிஞராய்ச்
   > சென்று இரப்பர் ஓர் இடத்துக் கூழ் எனின், செல்வம்
   > ஒன்றுஉண்டாக வைக்கற்பாற்று அன்று.

2. Ever since the days of immaculate wealth
   It never sticks on for ever in its apex but
   Will undergo as if in a cart wheel
   Hence share the agro-food with others.

   Well-gotten wealth out of peasantry should be spent for the benefit of poor and the indigent. The reason being that wealth by any means would never be with the earner for ever but will rotate in ups and downs as if in the wheel of fortune. Wealth by honest means should be spent on charitable deeds; by dishonest means is not assured of its longevity.

> துகள் தீர் பெருஞ் செல்வம் தோன்றியக்கால் தொட்டு
> பகடு நடந்த கூழ் பல்லாரோடு உண்க-
> அகடு உற யார் மாட்டும் நில்லாது. செல்வம்
> சகடக்கால் போல வரும்!

3. Those with canopy on the pachyderms
   And led an array of soldiers
   By a streak of misfortune may fall down adrift
   With their better-half snatched by foes.

Even rulers who rode gorgeously on caparisoned elephants may tumble down one-day or other. On their ignominious defeat and death, their wives may even be forced to go along with the victor.

Victorious king marry the daughter or wife of the vanquished ruler had been a custom in ancient days. Hence one must be aware that material wealth is neither stable nor permanent.

> யானை எருத்தம் பொலிய, குடை நிழற்கீழ்ச்
> சேனைத் தலைவராய்ச் சென்றோரும், ஏனை
> வினை உலப்ப, வேறு ஆகி வீழ்வர், தாம் கொண்ட
> மனையாளை மாற்றார் கொள.

4. Realize that those who are alive are not static;
   Arise to act hence amicably and homely;
   Life long days will soon be gone
   God of death is hastily coming soon.

Doing good therefore is a benevolent act. In this temporal life which is neither static nor endless, men should serve fellow beings and share with them the wealth they have. This they are meant to do before Yama, the god of death snatches their life.

No one can predict the arrival of Yama. His vicious technique is sometimes to catch hold of the victims unaware. Hence, do good to others.

> 'நின்றன நின்றன நில்லா' என உணர்ந்து,
> ஒன்றின ஒன்றின வல்லே, செயின், செய்க-
> சென்றன சென்றன, வாழ்நாள்; செறுத்து, உடன்
> வந்தது வந்தது, கூற்று!

5. If got anything worthwhile in hand,
   Hold it not for days together for
   Those who spent benevolently get rescued from
   Dry and dreary path, when God of death leads them
   on.

Whatever wealth a person has, shouldn't be hoarded, and be lain dormant presuming that the entire excessive lot must be set apart for future. Donating it for the poor and the needy will certainly smoothen the way that leads to doomsday, omitting the dreary path.

> என்னானும் ஒன்று தம் கையுறப் பெற்றக்கால்,
> பின் ஆவது என்று பிடித்து இரார், முன்னே
> கொடுத்தார் உயப் போவர்-கோடு இல் தீக் கூற்றம்.
> தொடுத்து ஆறு செல்லும் சுரம்.

6. Doomsday destined will never exceed the limit
   No body can escape the clutches of the God of
                                               death
   So be liberal to offer to others O! wealthy ! May
   Tomorrow be heard the sound of elegiac drum!

Human life on this earth is transitory. One's day of death cannot either be cancelled or get extended. Longevity is not unlimited. Hence the wealthy people are counseled to be liberal and generous. This is all the more important in life. The poet believes in destinarian philosophy.

இழைத்த நாள் எல்லை இகவா; பிழைத்து ஒரீஇ,
கூற்றம் குதித்து உய்ந்தார் ஈங்கு இல்லை;-ஆற்றப்
பெரும் பொருள் வைத்தீர்!-வழங்குமின்; நாளைத்
'தழீஇம் தழீஇம்' தண்ணம் படும்.

7. Gleaming sun as a measure all along daily
   God of death calculates and consumes your days;
   Do offer charities, be blessed and if not
   Even after you're born, ye will be deemed unborn.

Holding the sun as a measure, God of Death calculates your days. Before he takes you off, do help to others. If not, you will be deemed unborn. Purport of this poem is comparable to that of Kural-344. It boasts itself as day' if properly understood, it is a knife daily cuts away a portion from the life. Instability of life continues to be a theme to constantly urge the importance of extending charitable activities to the poor and deserving.

தோற்றம் சால் ஞாயிறு நாழியா, வைகலும்
கூற்றம் அளந்து, நும் நாள் உண்ணும்; ஆற்ற
அறம் செய்து அருளுடையீர் ஆகுமின்; யாரும்
பிறந்தும், பிறவாதாரில்.

8. Even huge wealth, of those petty minded, who consider
   With pride, I am rich and disrespectful wherever he goes,
   Will twinkle like lightning for a while from dark clouds'
   And get disappeared and uprooted for ever.

Wealth, of those who feel proud of their inherited richness, will vanish like lightning. Implication is that hence, one should do help to others before that wealth disappears.

Whoever is rich either by heredity or by self-efforts must be humble and respectful. If he behaves arrogantly with others in a mean and petty minded pride and arrogance, his wealth will disappear as swiftly as lightning from dark clouds.

> 'செல்வர் யாம்!' என்று தாம் செல்வுழி எண்ணாத
> புல்லறிவாளர் பெருஞ் செல்வம், எல்லில்
> கருங் கொண்மூ வாய் திறந்த மின்னுப்போல் தோன்றி
> மருங்கு அறக் கெட்டுவிடும்.

9. Neither enjoys nor majestical, earn not a glory
   Wipe not misery of kin and doesn't apportion
   But simply hoards and guards his wealth
   Alas! He will be deemed to be a loser.

Those who are resourceful and wealthy should rightly enjoy palatable food, clothing and a comfortable life on the one hand and spend money to perpetuate their image, assist kith and kin besides helping the poor. Not doing all these virtuous activities but inanely hoarding the wealth is either useless or render him unworthy of wealth and of any benefit out of it.

> உண்ணான், ஒளி நிறான், ஓங்கு புகழ் செய்யான்,
> துன்னருங் கேளிர் துயர் களையான், கொன்னே
> வழங்கான் பொருள் காத்து இருப்பானேல், 'அஆ!
> இழந்தான்' என்று எண்ணப்படும்.

10. Neither eat nor dress richly but wearily working
    Doesn't do lasting benevolence nor does offer aid
    But earn and hoard oh! The Lord of sky-scraping hills
    They will lose as bees their honey from the hive.

Those who simply hoard their wealth but still continue to go on earning without spending it on right means will lose their money either in dacoity or theft at one stroke are alike bees that gather honey all along for many days but lose it on a single day. Similar will be the end of hoarded wealth.

Loss of honey by the bees is an apt comparison to the deprivation of wealth the hoarders endure. Hunters will prepare a burning stick and show it around the beehive in the wild or on the branches of trees. Bees fly away leaving behind their honey to be taken away by the raiders. Loss of honey is compared to the loss of hoarded wealth.

> உடாஅதும், உண்ணாதும், தம் உடம்பு செற்றும்,
> கெடாஅத நல் அறமும் செய்யார், கொடாஅது
> வைத்து ஈட்டினார் இழப்பர்; வான் தோய் மலை நாட!
> உய்த்து ஈட்டும் தேனீக் கரி.

Chapter 2 - Instability of youth
***

The second Chapter deals with the inconstancy of the adolescent period. Its coverage is between the sixteenth year of one's age to about thirtieth. A period that entangles the youth into amorous activities. To undergo and enjoy sensual pleasures, what is primarily needed is wealth and along with it, a period of energetic youth. Hence, to deal with them in order, the instability of wealth has been taken up in the First Chapter and presently an account of the inconstancy of youth.

11. Conscious of grey hair in life, the wise men
    Relinquish excess of passions even in youth;
    Those who indulged in it sensually render themselves
    So weak as to get up laboriously with a stick.

Being conscious that avarice, passion and sensual pleasures hasten the oldness and grey hair, wise men avoid the excess of them, but those who unwarily indulge in them become so old and weak as to require a stick to stand up and walk.

Instead of getting involved in passionate behaviour, young men should adapt themselves to intelligence, sobriety and wiseness.

> 'நரை வரும்!' என்று எண்ணி, நல் அறிவாளர்
> குழவியிடத்தே துறந்தார்; புரை தீரா,
> மன்னா இளமை மகிழ்ந்தாரே, கோல் ஊன்றி
> இன்னாங்கு எழுந்திருப்பார்.

12. Intimacy got snapped, loved ones lessened
    Bonds of love loosened but still you don't realize !
    What purpose does this life serve? Misery has come
    As much to those who entrapped in a sinking ship.

Kinship of relatives and friends will not be as deep as it was in the youthhood of an individual when he becomes old. Pity it is that when a person grows old, friendship, affection, kinship and love will go off. He shall have to weep as a person who remains in a shipwreck. Hence, men should take efforts to lead an ethical life.

> நட்புநார் அற்றன; நல்லாரும் அஃகினார்;
> அற்புத் தளையும் அவிழ்ந்தன; உள் காணாய்;
> வாழ்தலின், ஊதியம் என் உண்டாம்? வந்ததே,
> ஆழ் கலத்து அன்ன கலுழ்!

13. Those who cling on to lusty and amorous life
    Until words muffled, staggering with a stick
    Deprived of teeth and disowned by all
    Have no way of reaching a heavenly bliss.

Feeble voice, painful stammer, loss of teeth, and poor eyesight are the sure signs of old age, Hence, amorus life of young age should not be thought of as permanent. It is transient. Conjugal enjoyment is not condemned here but one is cautioned that he shouldn't indulge in excessive amorous life.

> சொல் தளர்ந்து, கோல் ஊன்றி, சோர்ந்த நடையினர் ஆய்,
> பல் கழன்று, பண்டம் பழிகாறும் இல்-செறிந்து
> காம நெறி படரும் கண்ணினார்க்கு இல்லையே
> ஏம நெறி படரும் ஆறு.

14. To see her who is bended, fragile, wobbly headed
    Tottered in walk and holds now a stick
    Which once her mother held and on seeing that
    Lustful men would feel embittered nostalgically.

Purport of the poem is to indicate a pitiful and grand old woman to those who are enamoured of young virgins that this old lady must have been of extreme charm and beauty once but now has come to a miserable old age, implying thereby that youth hood is instable.

The abstract of the poem is that if only men realize the seminal truth that beauty and charm of today will not be the same tomorrow, they would not be lusty and lascivious.

> தாழா, தளரா, தலை நடுங்கா, தண்டு ஊன்றா,
> வீழா இறக்கும் இவள்மாட்டும், காழ் இலா
> மம்மர் கொள் மாந்தர்க்கு அணங்கு ஆகும் தன்கைக் கோல்
> அம்மனைக் கோல் ஆகிய ஞான்று.

15. The one who was my mother left me herein
    Gone in search of a mother who in turn
    If had done the same, pitiful is the world
    In making one mother to go after another.

My mother gone in search of another means that my mother after her death will be born again as a child. Thereby she will have a mother in the next birth. Based on the *Migration of soul Theory,* the poem attempts to explain that youth hood and at length human life is not static but replaced by old age and death. William Wordsworth's *Ode on the Intimations of Immortality* is, in a way comparable to this poem.

> எனக்குத் தாய் ஆகியாள் என்னை ஈங்கு இட்டு,
> தனக்குத் தாய் நாடியே சென்றாள்; தனக்குத் தாய்
> ஆகியவளும் அதுஆனால், தாய்த் தாய்க்கொண்டு,
> ஏகும் அளித்து, இவ் உலகு.

16. Triviality of a goat in munching green leaves of
    A garland that is to be put on it before it is sacrificed
    By a possessed priest in front of the anvil,
    Is not to be found among the wise men of wisdom.

Pity it is that a goat chews the leaves from a garland meant for donning it on its neck. Blissfully unaware that it was to be sacrificed on the anvil to propitiate rural deity. Such bleak innocence and unwariness of a goat is not to be seen among wisemen; because they are fully aware of inconstancy of the youth. They won't be vulnerable to the temptations of youth hood.

> வெறி அயர் வெங் களத்து வேல்மகன் பாணி
> முறி ஆர் நறுங் கண்ணி முன்னர்த் தயங்க,
> மறி குளகு உண்டன்ன மன்னா மகிழ்ச்சி
> அறிவுடையாளர்கண் இல்.

17. Youth hood is like trees deprived of their fruit
    In an orchard grown amidst green copse;
    Don't be enamored hence of this flashy eyed beauty
    She may be hunching soon with a stick in hand.

Youth hood of human beings is likened to a tree deprived of its fruits. Keeping this instability of youth in mind, don't be desirous of young girls and speak of their eyes as sharp as spear. She may become aged and hunch-backed in the days to come.

> பனி படு சோலைப் பயன் மரம் எல்லாம்
> கனி உதிர்ந்து வீழ்ந்தற்று, இளமை; 'நனி பெரிதும்
> வேல் கண்ணள்!' என்று இவளை வெஃகன்மின்; மற்றுஇவளும்
> கோல் கண்ணள் ஆகும், குனிந்து.

18. How old you are, what stage the teeth
    Haven't tasted victuals, hard and soft;
    Series of such queries darted at us
    Indicate that wisemen do not value the youth.

Enquiry of a man's health, stamina and stature indicate that the enquirer is very well aware that the old age is coming soon and the youth of a man is not constant but evanescent.

> 'பருவம் எனைத்து உள? பல்லின் பால் ஏனை?
> இரு சிகையும் உண்டீரோ?' என்று, வரிசையால்
> உள் நாட்டம் கொள்ளப்படுதலால், யாக்கைக் கோள்
> எண்ணார், அறிவுடையார்.

19. Think not, young I am, let me support later.
    But be charitable plainly while you're rich;
    Even when ripe-old fruits remain in branches
    Those unripe falling off in a gusty wind.

Implication is that as unripe fruits untimely fall down from its branches, even in youth, certain individuals may breathe their last. Young age is not stable and firm. Hence when one is resourceful and rich, he must extend charitable activities to the poor, indigent and needy.

> 'மற்று அறிவாம் நல் வினை; யாம் இளையம்' என்னாது,
> கைத்து உண்டாம் போழ்தே, கரவாது, அறம் செய்ம்மின்!
> முற்றி இருந்த கனி ஒழிய, தீ வளியால்
> நல் காய் உதிர்தலும் உண்டு!

20. True it's merciless Yama is after his due victims
    Snatches even immature foetus from wailing
                                                      mothers;
    Aware of his gamble, gather the bundle of good
                                                      deeds
    And get your eternal path charted blessedly.

God of death is on the prowl to snatch young and old and even foetus from the womb. Before that merciless leveller does his menace, go behind the good deeds, do them and relish a temporal bliss.

> ஆள் பார்த்து உழலும் அருள் இல் கூற்று உண்மையால்,
> தோள்கோப்புக் காலத்தால் கொண்டு உய்ம்மின்; பீள்
>   பிதுக்கிப்
> பிள்ளையைத் தாய் அலறக் கோடலால், மற்று அதன்
> கள்ளம் கடைப்பிடித்தல் நன்று.

☙ ❖ ❖ ❧

Chapter 3 - Instability of body
***

Human body is consisting of bone, muscle, skin, brain and blood. Movement of the body is possible, if only there is life and its vibrancy. Growth of any human body is clearly visible when a boy grows into youth hood. But that growth also may get lessened and restrained until the breath is stifled. Human life is provisional. Here follows therefore in ten stanzas, the instability of human body.

21. Even kings rode on elephants under royal canopy
    That resembles like full moon on a mountain-head
    Have been doomed of their death with impunity
    And nobody has been exempted from death
    inevitable.

A king can afford enormous expenditure to get him cured of even a chronic illness. But one day or other, he too has to die. It is informed here that death is invincible. Before that fatality occurs, do good things in life.

It may be recalled that an English Poet Shirley has titled a poem of hers-*Death, the Leveller.* It does not discriminate a king from a citizen nor does a rich from the poor.

> மலைமிசைத் தோன்றும் மதியம்போல், யானைத்
> தலைமிசைக் கொண்ட குடையர், நிலமிசைத்
> துஞ்சினார் என்று எடுத்துத் தூற்றப்பட்டார் அல்லால்,
> எஞ்சினார் இவ் உலகத்து இல்.

22. Resplendent sun as a measuring rod of life
    Arises everyday at dawn and hence
    Before your life dries off, be a benefactor;
    Whosoever you're, wouldn't be alive for ever.

The sun that rises every day is a measuring unit of life. In any one of the days in future, death is bound to come. No one will be alive forever. So what will alive posthumously in the world is the assistance and benefits that he extended to deserving persons.

In a different context what Shakespeare says is to be contrasted here.

The good that is often interred with the bones.
The evil that men do lives after them. - Julius Caesar

வாழ்நாட்கு அலகா, வயங்கு ஒளி மண்டிலம்
வீழ் நாள் படாஅது எழுதலால், வாழ்நாள்
உலவாமுன் ஒப்புரவு ஆற்றுமின்; யாரும்
நிலவார், நிலமிசை மேல்.

23. Dulcet symphonies reverberate on marital eve
    May sound ominously as death knell on the same
                                                day;
    Realising this risk, the thoughts of great men
    Would go ahead by tracking the blessed path.

Though not often, once in a way, totally in unexpected circumstances, a marriage may even go topsy turvy into a mourning event. Life is not static but trivial and transitory. Hence well informed and knowledgeable persons will attune themselves to the path that is spiritually harmonious. Blessed path-renunciation.

'மன்றம் கறங்க மணப் பறை ஆயின,
அன்று அவர்க்கு ஆங்கே, பிணப் பறை ஆய், பின்றை
ஒலித்தலும் உண்டாம்' என்று, உய்ந்துபோம் ஆறே
வலிக்குமாம்-மாண்டார் மனம்.

24. Beat the drum, first to condole the death
    Slightly after when they beat it again, note it well
    Closing the fire-pot in a tripod, those who are yet to
                                                die
    Will proceed carrying the already dead to cremation.

A dead person is carried to grave by those who are yet to die. Cremation of the body is customarily done among the Tamils. Either a son or a cousin will proceed along with the mourners by carrying the fiery sticks in an earthen - ware to lit the pyre. This is to indicate the instability of human body in worldly life.

> சென்றே எறிப ஒருகால்; சிறு வரை
> நின்றே எறிப, பறையினை; நன்றேகாண்,
> முக் காலைக் கொட்டினுள், மூடி, தீக் கொண்டு எழுவர்,
> செத்தாரைச் சாவார் சுமந்து!

25. Relatives in group gather and sob bitterly
    On seeing a corpse being carried to the grave;
    But to those who unwarily relish the conjugal
                                              felicity
    The drum-beats of obsequies will indicate eternal
                                              truth.

Indication of the instability of human body is eternal truth. In the Tamil original, the third and the fourth line defy typical translation as they are rhythmic and onomatopoeic. As they operate at the lexical level, they cannot be translated. Beating of drum is a custom in merry making festivities as well as on the mourning. But the drummers will orchestrate the beating in such a way that one could differentiate even at an audible distance whether the event is joyful or sorrowful.

> கணம் கொண்டு சுற்றத்தார் கல்லென்று அலற,
> பிணம் கொண்டு காட்டு உய்ப்பார்க் கண்டும், மணம்
>   கொண்டு, ஈண்டு,
> 'உண்டு, உண்டு, உண்டு' என்னும் உணர்வினான் -
>   சாற்றுமே,
> 'டொண் டொண் டொண்' என்னும் பறை.

26. When life, like an acrobat hold and manipulate
					dance
    In a body which is a pouch of skin, goes off
    What does it matter, if the corpse is dragged on or
					buried off
    Or thrown off elsewhere or if it's condemned off?

Addressed to those who ritually decorate the dead body before effecting a burial. Human body is known for its inconstancy and destructibility. But still certain unwise men are very fond of their body. Even after its death, the action of decorating the corpse reiterate foolishness. It makes no sense whether the body is dragged or buried or thrown about.

The custom among the Jews is to throw away the corpse amidst the bushes to be devoured by vultures and eagles.

> நார்த் தொடுத்து ஈர்க்கில் என்? நன்று ஆய்ந்து அடக்கில் என்?
> பார்த்துழிப் பெய்யில் என்? பல்லோர் பழிக்கில் என்?
> தோற்பையுள்நின்று, தொழில் அறச் செய்து ஊட்டும்
> கூத்தன் புறப்பட்டக்கால்.

27. As bubbles appear and burst at once in pouring
					rains
    The human body is speedily perishable;
    Those strong who unwaveringly realize this, are
					the wise,
    Who else can equal these very great men?

Human body is as brittle as bubbles that break in downpour. Those who are aware of this are wisemen. What the stanza implies is those wise men would extend charitable activities, once they realize that human life is, as unstable and perishable as the bubbles that appear and disappear during torrential downpour. Those who realise this and do good deeds in this life are unequalled and great.

'படு மழை மொக்குளின் பல் காலும் தோன்றி,
கெடும், இது ஓர் யாக்கை' என்று எண்ணி, 'தடுமாற்றம்
தீர்ப்பேம் யாம்' என்று உணரும் திண் அறிவாளரை
நேர்ப்பார் யார், நீள் நிலத்தின்மேல்?

28. Those endowed with a strong physique
    Grapple the joy spiritual with the healthy body
    Which may, appear as roaming cloud on the mount
    And may leave off its life as much as the cloud
    vanish.

The human frame is transient, in a way. No less is one's birth, growth and death. They go off as the clouds vanish when they are up above the mountains. Before such a short-lived body expires, men should strive for a spiritual bliss. This is a note of persuasion to do benevolent things.

யாக்கையை யாப்புடைத்தாப் பெற்றவர், தாம் பெற்ற
யாக்கையால் ஆய பயன் கொள்க-யாக்கை
மலை ஆடும் மஞ்சுபோல் தோன்றி, மற்று ஆங்கே
நிலையாது நீத்துவிடும்!

29. Unstable dews on the blade of grass
    Is our body and hence perform acts
    Charitable now itself as the next of kin sobbingly
    Might say, Here he was, lying, dying and gone off.

Somebody would surprisingly say, just now I saw him but now deceased, others would shockingly observe, he was in bed just an hour earlier but now dead. When everyone says so, it is obvious that the instability of human life is realized by one and all. Hence it behoves us to do benevolent acts without any more delay.

'புல் நுனிமேல் நீர்போல் நிலையாமை' என்று எண்ணி,
இன்னினியே செய்க அறவினை-'இன்னினியே
நின்றான், இருந்தான், கிடந்தான், தன் கேள் அலறச்
சென்றான்' எனப்படுதலால்!

30. As birds leave the nests of the branches
    And fly aloft to go to a place at a distance,
    Persons uninvitedly born of a womb
    As kins of a family and leave the body off.

It is incumbent on human beings, therefore to do benevolent and charitable activities for the sake of others who are in dire need of help. Otherwise no sooner the resourceful persons are dead than their body is put into fire until it is burnt to ashes.

> கேளாதே வந்து, கிளைகளாய் இல் தோன்றி,
> வாளாதே போவரால், மாந்தர்கள்-வாளாதே.
> சேக்கை மரன் ஒழியச் சேண் நீங்கு புள் போல,
> யாக்கை தமர்க்கு ஒழிய நீத்து.

ஓ ♦ ❖ ♦ ஒ

Chapter 4 - Reiterate Ethics
***

Ethical behavior is not only essential but also practicable if only we have a will in this temporal life. It is not destructible as wealth, youth and human body. Hence as a noble virtue it warrants a separate chapter of ten stanzas.

31. Beneficiaries of past deeds but unethical in next
    Are born anew as destitute and suffer
    By having been ejected out in backyards
    Of the rich whose mansions they look despairingly.

Those who were charitable in their previous birth, enjoy happy temporal life. If they are unethical now, they are bound to born as destitute and made to look towards the rich for support. If this is the net result of their un ethicality and pride, what is expected of us by the moral science is that we must be benevolent, ethical, virtuous and charitable.

> 'அகத்து ஆரே வாழ்வார்?' என்று அண்ணாந்து நோக்கி,
> புகத் தாம் பெறாஅர், புறங்கடை பற்றி,
> மிகத் தாம் வருந்தியிருப்பரே-மேலைத்
> தவத்தால் தவம் செய்யாதார்.

32. Passionate of wealth, becoming rich
    Tend to forget charity, O! Mind
    So far led your life with all such efforts and
    Spent likewise hitherto but what to be done
                                                         hereafter.

This poem is purported to have addressed to human mind. This temporal life you have attuned towards earning only, forgetting charity and piety. Life has been spent almost in this way and inform me now what you are going to do hereafter.

Implication is that one should be charitable without waiting for an occasion.

> 'ஆவாம் நாம், ஆக்கம் நசைஇ; அறம் மறந்து,
> போவாம் நாம்' என்னா,-புலை நெஞ்சே!-ஓவாது
> நின்று உஞற்றி வாழ்தி எனினும், நின் வாழ்நாள்கள்
> சென்றன; செய்வது உரை.

33. When Destiny brings in misery, the unwise
    Disquietened of their mind, heaves a sigh;
    Those who realize it's the resultant effect
    Of previous birth, by-pass the bounds of misery.

Even amidst suffering which is the effect of previous birth, one should continue to help the poor and the needy; otherwise he would suffer in the forthcoming birth also. Ethical life is thus reiterated in this stanza.

> வினைப் பயன் வந்தக்கால், வெய்ய உயிரா,
> மனத்தின் அழியுமாம், பேதை; நினைத்து, அதனைத்
> தொல்லையது என்று உணர்வாரே தடுமாற்றத்து
> எல்லை இகந்து ஒருவுவார்.

34. With the benefit of having had rare human body
    Do in large measure the act of charity;
    To enable rebirth as juice out of sugarcane
    While body as bagasse will be left out.

Men are bound to help others before their life expires because the charity they do will render a sweet effect as much as the juice of a sugarcane but the body as its solid waste will get destroyed.

> அரும் பெறல் யாக்கையைப் பெற்ற பயத்தால்,
> பெரும் பயனும் ஆற்றவே கொள்க!-கரும்பு ஊர்ந்த
> சாறுபோல் சாலவும் பின் உதவி, மற்று அதன்
> கோதுபோல் போகும், உடம்பு!

35. Men get sugar cubes after crushing canes
    Won't regret when its bagasse burning as fuel;
    Those who suffered their life in noble charities
    Won't be bitter when god of death comes.

Those who have done good deeds in life would not be fearful of death. Substance of this poem resembles a typical rural scene. Farmers cultivate sugarcane and get it crushed at the appointed time. The Cane-Waste, known as bagasse that accumulates hugely will be burnt in the process of boiling the sugar juice. No regrets for burning it. Similarly those who suffer in life to do charities won't groan and feel bitter at the time of death. Because they are fully conscious that their benevolent activities would bring in better rebirth as juice from cane and hence their death is not a botheration for them.

> கரும்பு ஆட்டி, கட்டி சிறுகாலைக் கொண்டார்
> துரும்பு எழுந்து வேங்கால் துயர் ஆண்டு உழவார்;
> வருந்தி உடம்பின் பயன் கொண்டார், கூற்றம்
> வருங்கால் பரிவது இலர்.

36. Unmindful, if death arrives now or day before
    Or at any time but assuming it's just behind you
    Avoid sinful deeds and do maximum possible
    Benevolent actions as counseled by elders.

What is warranted by the poet is that there shall be no delay in doing benevolent activities, unmindful of the arrival of death. Assuming that the death is just behind you to snatch you off at any time of the day, do your good deeds as advised by the elders in society.

> 'இன்றுகொல்? அன்றுகொல்? என்றுகொல்?' என்னாது,
> 'பின்றையே நின்றது கூற்றம்' என்று எண்ணி,
> ஒருவுமின், தீயவை; ஒல்லும் வகையால்
> மருவுமின், மாண்டார் அறம்.

37. If analyse bodily actions performed and
    Benevolent in the world they are more and hence
    Instead of using them for the body only
    Do something amenable for the world celestial.

Even though there are many useful, happy and benevolent actions are performed by our human body in the world what is insisted here is that those actions have to be oriented towards charity and kindness to make us eligible to gain an entry into heaven.

> மக்களால் ஆய பெரும் பயனும், ஆயுங்கால்,
> எத்துணையும் ஆற்றப் பலஆனால், தொக்க
> உடம்பிற்கே ஒப்புரவு செய்து ஒழுகாது, உம்பர்க்
> கிடந்து உண்ணப் பண்ணப்படும்.

38. A tiny banyan seed grown all around
    Provides shadow massively and as such
    Even though small a gift if given to great men
    Would grow widespread even wider than the sky.

Banyan seed, though very small would grow gradually into a huge tree and provides shadow massively in a large area. Similarly if the gift or an aid given to virtuous persons is very small, it would disseminate its benevolence to a very great extent. So, one has to be charitable and kind. It is not the quantity that counts. But the quality and timeliness.

> உறக்கும் துணையது ஓர் ஆலம் வித்து ஈண்டி,
> இறப்ப நிழல் பயந்தாஅங்கு, அறப்பயனும்,
> தான் சிறிதுஆயினும், தக்கார் கைப் பட்டக்கால்,
> வான் சிறிதாப் போர்த்துவிடும்.

39. Realise not daily the extinction of days
    Overlooking that a day is gone off
    Happily presume it as a day real
    Not knowing that it reduces the life span.

The Tamil original of this poem-39 in *Naladiyar* is a rhetorical composition using the word 'vaigai' (daily) seven times in its four – lined venba metre. A rare feat of playing with words but cannot be typically and exactly translated. This stanza is comparable to a couplet in Thirukkural. I-34-4. Its purport is every day is not enjoyable. Realise it our life is like a sword.

> வகலும் வைகல் வரக்கண்டும், அஃது உணரார்,
> வைகலும், வைகலை வைகும் என்று இன்புறுவர்
> வைகலும் வைகல் தம் வாழ்நாள்மேல் வைகுதல்
> வைகலை வைத்து உணராதார்.

40. Setting aside the gem of dignity and I 'could lead
    A base and degraded life so abjectly, by feeding it
    If only the body is sure of longevity
    And continue to be alive very strongly.

The poem a first-person narrative implies that the human body cannot be sure of longevity however much it is fed sumptuously even by losing one's own honour and dignity. If so why should I beg and develop the body? Hence the poet's counseling is that to nurture the human body which is not constant and durable, one should not degrade himself to an abject and dishonorable living.

> மான அருங் கலம் நீக்கி, இரவு என்னும்
> ஈன இளிவினால் வாழ்வேன்மன்-ஈனத்தால்
> ஊட்டியக் கண்ணும் உறுதி சேர்ந்து, இவ் உடம்பு
> நீட்டித்து நிற்கும் எனின்!

Chapter 5 - Non-Purity
***

The human body is destructible and not pure unless it is kept hygienic and clean. It has to be deemed a trough of trash even though it is described as soft and tender. The degenerative and decadent human body is derisively spoken of in these ten stanzas. Learned men should not be mindful of being lustful but think in terms of ethics and morality.

Here the term 'purity' is an oblique reference to celibacy that does not mean this word is an advocacy of absolute renunciation, since its second Division speaks about the moral life of householders. What this chapter aims to say is that one should not be passionate and excessive in carnal pleasures.

41. Great men flatteringly speaks of the lass
    As young, soft and tender, do not realize that body
    A trough that needs a stick to drive the crow
    When even minuscule of skin gets scratched.

When a scratch or a wound is open in skin, even a crow may attempt to peck it. A stick may be needed to drive it away. Such is the decadence of skin. Enamoured of its colour and softness as much as that of tender mango leaves, men begin flattering young woman. If only they realize that not only the skin but also human body is like a trough of trash, they would not be lusty.

> மாக் கேழ் மட நல்லாய்!' என்று அரற்றும் சான்றவர்
> நோக்கார்கொல், நொய்யது ஓர் துச்சிலை? யாக்கைக்கு ஓர்
> ஈச் சிறகு அன்னது ஓர் தோல் அறினும், வேண்டுமே,
> காக்கை கடிவது ஓர் கோல்!

42. Outer covering is skin, orifices many but hiding
 All of these is a body with an attire fair
 But not exactly fair, doesn't deserve endearing
 words
 But to be viewed as a bag is seen upside down.

Condemnation of human body is lucid and picturesque in this stanza. Setting aside the outward attire, jewels and charm of the body, look at it as a bag stitched is seen upside down. Then only the non-appreciable reality will be obvious. When the bag is looked at its inner - side, the stitching line and residual pieces of cloth will be found. But in its outer, the bag will be fine. Orifices include two eyes, two ears, two nostrils, mouth and anus.

தோற் போர்வைமேலும் துளை பலவாய், பொய்ம்
மறைக்கும்
மீப் போர்வை மாட்சித்து, உடம்பு; ஆனால், மீப் போர்வை
பொய்ம் மறையா, காமம் புகலாது, மற்று அதனைப்
பைம் மறியாப் பார்க்கப்படும்.

43. Great men firmly give up infatuation for ever;
 Know what's eaten remains in body as dirt; will
 They forsake that firmness for a deceptive show
 Of flower - laden head and perfume spiced mouth?

No. It is believed that great men would not allow themselves to be seduced by women. Adolescent women decorate themselves attractively with fabrics, flowers and perfumes. They chew scented nuts and betel. But learned men, who gave up lust will never be infatuated by these outward attractions.

தக்கோலம் தின்று, தலை நிறையப் பூச் சூடி,
பொய்க் கோலம் செய்ய, ஒழியுமே'எக்காலும்
உண்டி வினையுள் உறைக்கும்' எனப் பெரியோர்
கண்டு, கைவிட்ட மயல்.

44. Will I be enticed of what unwise say that
    Eyes of women are alike *kuvalai*, fish and spear?
    I shall continue to be stern and mindful of reality
    Of eyes that appear to be sockets after uprooting
                                     the Palmyra fruits.

This is the first-person narrative of the poet. Customary among the learned men is to compare the cheerful eyes of ladies to bluish kuvalai flower, to the briskness of fishes and to the sharpness of spear. But those eyes, devoid of watery substance would appear to be sunken, dry and dreary. Not to be tempted by them.

This poem is purported to have been addressed by a stern-minded realist. Much against the sensuous attraction towards ladies, he affirms that he is not merely terrestrial but mindful of things celestial and eternal.

'தெள் நீர்க் குவளை, பொரு கயல், வேல்' என்று,
கண் இல் புன்மாக்கள் கவற்ற, விடுவெனோ
உள் நீர் களைந்தக்கால் நுங்கு சூன்றிட்டன்ன
கண் நீர்மை கண்டு ஒழுகுவேன்.

45. Will I be seduced of what the ignorant babblers say
    That teeth of women are alike mullai buds and
                                     pearl?
    I shall behave sternly after noticing the broken
                                     teeth of
    Bones visibly strewn around in graveyards.

Having seen teeth and bones scattered around in the graveyards, I got myself attracted to renunciation. Never would I give it up, even after hearing the ignorant prattlers who say that the teeth of women are comparable to *mullai* buds and white pearls. The verbal appreciation of outward beauty cannot wean me away from my desire toward celestial blessing.

'முல்லை முகை, முறுவல், முத்து' என்று இவை பிதற்றும்
கல்லாப் புன்மாக்கள் கவற்ற விடுவெனோ
எல்லாரும் காண, புறங்காட்டு உதிர்ந்து உக்க
பல்-என்பு கண்டு ஒழுகுவேன்.

46. To which shall the soft garlanded lady be
                                    categorized
    When she, in her body contains liver and flesh
    Besides blood and bone bound up with
    Nerves amidst a lot of muscles covered by skin?

A lady has no distinctive quality of femininity in her excepting the physical combination of liver, flesh, blood, bone and skin. Such indistinctiveness of feminine gender is in no way appreciable and hence men who are devoted to blessed life of eternity should not be enamoured of the physical side of female body.

குடரும், கொழுவும், குருதியும், என்பும்,
தொடரும் நரம்பொடு தோலும், இடையிடையே
வைத்த தடியும், வழும்பும், ஆம் மற்று இவற்றுள்
எத் திறத்தாள், ஈர்ங் கோதையாள்?

47. Nauseating dirt semi-solid of nine orifices
    Gets squeezes out of her body but still
    Enticed by her skin, the one who speaks adoringly of
                                                      her
    Shoulders and bangles is an ignorant fool.

When an ignorant fool is said to be wide-eyed to admire the shoulders and bangles of a woman, its implication is that great men of talent would never succumb themselves to that decadent beauty. Surface level exterior beauty is meant to be decayed and hence great men would resist them forcefully and begin mindful of eternal bliss.

ஊறி, உவர்த்தக்க ஒன்பது வாய்ப் புலனும்
கோதிக் குழம்பு அலைக்கும் கும்பத்தை, பேதை,
'பெருந்தோளி! பெய்வளாய்!' என்னும்-மீப் போர்த்த
கருந் தோலால் கண் விளக்கப்பட்டு.

48. Aren't they aware her body is degraded but celebrated
For its being fragrant of sandal and garland?
When that sweaty body is dead like an axle-broken cart
Vultures of every kind peck and swallow that corpse.

There are certain people enamoured of young ladies who decorate their body with incense and garland. Ignorant of its being a fleshy body and gets itself pecked and swallowed by eagles after its death, they celebrate it. Let them not do it but devote themselves to penance and enjoy the bliss of heavenly paradise.

பண்டம் அறியார், படு சாந்தும் கோதையும்
கண்டு, பாராட்டுவார் கண்டிலர்கொல்-மண்டிப்
பெடைச் சேவல் வன் கழுகு பேர்த்து இட்டுக் குத்தல்,
முடைச் சாகாடு அச்சு இற்றுழி.

49. Skulls of the deceased, fearful to look at
With dry socket of eyes mockingly implying
Those alive should follow virtuous path of the dead
And seemingly say that this is the nature of human
life.

The white - colour skulls with open teeth and hollow eyes of burnt out corpses would be fearful to look at. The poet imagines that the skulls appear to be silently warning the people that this will be the net result of human life. It implies therefore that mankind should follow ethical way of life instead of clinging to the sensuous aspirations in human life.

கழிந்தார் இடு தலை, கண்டார் நெஞ்சு உட்க,
குழிந்து ஆழ்ந்த கண்ணவாய்த் தோன்றி, ஒழிந்தாரை,
'போற்றி நெறி நின்மின்; இற்று, இதன் பண்பு' என்று
சாற்றும்கொல், சாலச் சிரித்து!

50. White skulls of the dead, laugh frighteningly to
Avoid the offence of arrogance; those who rid of this
Aware the quality of life is this piteousness of a body;
So, never they would attribute value to it.

Ephemeral value of human body the learned know and hence instead of giving importance to it, they would seek eternal pleasure and spiritual glory. This is to be contrasted with what *Saint Tirumoolar* says, I have grown and nurtured the body because the life is nurtured by the body. For the sake of life I cannot but safeguard the body.

உயிர் போயார் வெண் தலை உட்கச் சிரித்து,
செயிர் தீர்க்கும், செம்மாப்பவரை; செயிர் தீர்ந்தார்
கண்டு, 'இற்று, இதன் வண்ணம்' என்பதனால், தம்மை ஓர்
பண்டத்துள் வைப்பது இலர்.

Chapter 6 - Renunciation
***

Renunciation is an act of giving up certain pleasures for moral or religious reasons. A sense of inner feeling of proudness or haughtiness has also to be given up as an undesirable quality. An endearment of wealth and power is not desirable because they are the external enticements. Men of spirituality shun and avoid internal passion and external avarice.

51. As darkness goes off at the advent of a lamp
    Sin dares not before one's own penance;
    Evil envelops when benevolence is given up
    As gloominess gets in when ghee is burnt.

Any action against the laws of God is sin; also against social approval. But the deleterious effect of sin cannot stand before penance or the benevolent deeds of an individual. When these noble actions are stopped, the effect of evil will envelop him as darkness slowly gets into the room when the ghee is gradually burnt in a lamp.

விளக்குப் புக இருள் மாய்ந்தாங்கு, ஒருவன்
தவத்தின்முன் நில்லாதாம் பாவம்; விளக்கு நெய்
தேய்விடத்துச் சென்று இருள் பாய்ந்தாங்கு, நல் வினை
தீர்விடத்து நிற்குமாம், தீது.

52. Wise men would do actions objectively
    Aware of ailment, agedness and death at length;
    Unwise are like madmen vainly prattle about
    As if music and astrology are means to an end.

Those who are conscious of the inconstancy of this temporal life, devote themselves to actions of nobility and spirituality. Others who are unwise enjoy sensual life in music and entertainment. Also consult astrology to calculate their longevity, unaware of the transitoriness of life.

The poet doesn't seem to give credence to astrology which has become a questionable subject nowadays credible or not.

> நிலையாமை, நோய், மூப்பு, சாக்காடு, என்று எண்ணி,
> தலையாயார் தம் கருமம் செய்வார்; தொலைவு இல்லாச்
> சத்தமும் சோதிடமும் என்று ஆங்கு இவை பிதற்றும்
> பித்தரின் பேதையார் இல்.

53. Aware of instability of domestic life, youth hood charm, beauty, majesticity, wealth and strength
    Learned will hold a holy man as guide
    And seek renunciation from worldly life.

Disowning worldly life does not seem to have been a self-styled vocation of penance and piety. Traditionally novices in spiritual life sought the help and direction of ascetics to lead a life of renunciation.

> இல்லம், இளமை, எழில், வனப்பு, மீக்கூற்றம்,
> செல்வம், வலி, என்று இவை எல்லாம், மெல்ல,
> நிலையாமை கண்டு, நெடியார், துறப்பர்
> தலையாயர்-தாம் உய்யக் கொண்டு.

54. Poor men relish a little domestic pleasure.
    Despite multitudiness of misery in householding;
    Hence aware of the sufferings in family life
    The learned give it up in favour of renunciation.

This stanza gives an impression that for all individuals, the act of renouncing life is far better than family life. Strictly speaking one should undergo a life of penance only after spending a good portion of his family life and that too after exhausting lust and other carnal pleasures. This is what Tolkappiam says as a virtue of ancient Tamils. The 'Sanyasam' is recommended only after leading a family life. But modern Hindu religion and Roman

Catholicism in Christianity impose celibacy and do not permit family life for those who baptize into sainthood. This is against natural law of life and hence celibacy is broken and violation is abound in both these and similar other religions.

> துன்பம் பல நாள் உழந்தும், ஒரு நாளை
> இன்பமே காமுறுவர், ஏழையார்; இன்பம்
> இடை தெரிந்து, இன்னாமை நோக்கி, மனை ஆறு
> அடைவு ஒழிந்தார், ஆன்று அமைந்தார்.

55. Youthhood has gone off vainly and soon
    To follow the ailments and old age! O mind!
    Devoid of following me, you're going ahead
    Accompany me towards a path benevolent.

   The poem is purported to have been said by an individual to his mind. The mind is infatuated with worldly life presuming it as permanent, unaware of the fact that initial youthhood has gone already off. Ailments and old age are meant to follow soon. Unmindful of these setbacks, mind leads him towards materialistic wordly life. Hence he counsels it to make an attempt to seek a benevolent liberation from worldly bonds.

   An individual guided himself to youthful aspirations, subsequently realized that what all he had done was in vain. Perhaps reminding himself of an adage, Better late than never, he counsels his mind that hereafter at least, he must strive for a life of penance.

> கொன்னே கழிந்தன்று இளமையும்! இன்னே
> பிணியொடு மூப்பும் வருமால்;- துணிவு ஒன்றி,
> என்னொடு சூழாது, எழுநெஞ்சே!- போதியோ,
> நல் நெறி சேர, நமக்கு?

56. Devoid of sterling qualities and barren too
    But still she can't be set aside by her husband;
    Marriage a Voluntary misery and so the learned
    Counsels us to avoid it to take up renunciation.

A wife proper was expected to be of good character and to beget children. In case, if she doesn't behave and bear heirs, she can't be neglected as per the norms of ancient society. A barren woman may prove to be an unavoidable burden. To avoid these botherations, learned people advise a restricted life of renunciation. Omission of onerous domesticity is hinted at. The custom of the Jains is to undertake renunciation even at an early age.

> 'மாண்ட குணத்தொடு மக்கட் பேறு இல் எனினும்,
> பூண்டான் கழித்தற்கு அருமையால், பூண்ட
> மிடி என்னும் காரணத்தின், மேன்முறைக்கண்ணே
> கடி' என்றார், கற்று அறிந்தார்.

57. When penance perseverely taken get broken
    And when overwhelming miseries exceed within
    Those who set them aside with a stoic mind
    Are those who safeguard the discipline of
                                            asceticism.

The power of hermits and those of penance is not only to bear the worldly miseries but also to throw them off and establish the discipline of recluses. Such hermits are the good-minded and benevolent persons.

> ஊக்கித் தாம் கொண்ட விரதங்கள் உள் உடைய,
> தாக்கு அரும் துன்பங்கள் தாம் தலைவந்தக்கால்,
> நீக்கி, நிறுஉம் உரவோரே, நல் ஒழுக்கம்
> காக்கும் திருவத்தவர்.

58. Duty of ascetics is not only to bear with
    The scorn but to feel pity for the scorner
    Whether he would be penalized in fiery hell
    As a sequence of having insulted the noble.

Seers and saints are expected to be not only tolerant when they are insulted. But also feel piteous whether the insulting person will be punished in hell for having shown the insult. Anger and annoyance shall be alien to the holy seers. This poem is in a way comparable to *Thirukkural - 987*.

> What fruit doth your perfection yield you, say?
> Unless to men who work you ill you good repay?

> தம்மை இகழ்ந்தமை தாம் பொறுப்பது அன்றி, 'மற்று
> எம்மை இகழ்ந்த வினைப் பயத்தான், உம்மை
> எரிவாய் நிரயத்து வீழ்வர்கொல்!' என்று
> பரிவதூஉம், சான்றோர் கடன்.

59. One who prevent excessive desire of five
    Organs, body, mouth, eyes, nose and ears
    From entangling the mind but directing it into
    Penance unfailingly attains heavenly bliss.

Desires arise through the five organs of the body. Any man who prevent these passions from ensnaring the mind but channeling them into the effect of renunciation is bound to reach heaven directly. Philosophers compare these five senses to hunters who fascinatingly bewilder the mind into materialistic passions.

> மெய், வாய், கண், மூக்கு, செவி எனப் பேர் பெற்ற
> ஐ வாய வேட்கை அவாவினை, கைவாய்,
> கலங்காமல் காத்து, உய்க்கும் ஆற்றல் உடையான்
> விலங்காது வீடு பெறும்.

60. Even if misery abounds, poor don't think of
    Renounce but enamoured of sensual pleasures;
    Whereas the wise realize a misery lurking
    In that every pleasure and so never desirous of it.

Carnal pleasures retain individuals in domestic life. Those men are unwise and materialistic. Setting aside these trivials, the wise men embrace ethical life. They are fully conscious that even within those domestic pleasures lie a misery melancholy and uneasiness. Hence their adherence to renunciation.

> துன்பமே மீதூரக் கண்டும், துறவு உள்ளார்,
> இன்பமே காமுறுவர், ஏழையார்; இன்பம்
> இசைதொறும், மற்று அதன் இன்னாமை நோக்கி,
> பசைதல் பரியாதாம், மேல்.

Chapter 7 - Absence of anger
***

If one is really an ethical person, he must bear anger even when it is incited against him. More so for the sages and saints because they are the examples and role models for others. Hence this chapter against anger comes successively after the renunciation of ascetics.

61. Let those who respect us and others who not only
    Disrespect but insult us be deemed as such;
    Even a fly that treads and sits on our head is not
    higher;
    Good it's so in not acutely wrathful at insults.

If low-bred and idiotic persons insult us, we should not be mindful of it. Take it easy and move ahead. Even a tiny fly sits on any part of our body and even on our head. Doesn't mean the tiny creature is in its higher level than men. Therefore insults from idiots and fools need not be acutely felt.

மதித்து இறப்பாரும் இறக்க! மதியார்,
மிதித்து இறப்பாரும் இறக்க! மிதித்து ஏறி,
ஈயும் தலைமேல் இருத்தலால், அஃது அறிவார்
காயும் கதம் இன்மை நன்று.

62. Even when insults prevent progressive steps
    Ascetics are courageous to fulfill their mission
    Will they give up the congenitally dignified life
    Without safeguarding it from any least insult?

No. Typical ascetics will never give up their life even when others infuriate or annoy them. Because their objective is noble, pious and devotional. They will safeguard their life to fulfil their missionary obligations. They will never be cowed down by any insult or annoyance.

தண்டாச் சிறப்பின் தம் இன் உயிரைத் தாங்காது,
கண்டுழி எல்லாம் துறப்பவோ-மண்டி,
அடி பெயராது, ஆற்ற இளி வந்த போழ்தின்
முடிகிற்கும் உள்ளத்தவர்?

63. Angry words, when one utters unguardedly
 Will hurt others constantly and hence
 Highly knowledgeable elders on any occasion
 Will never speak harsh words on anybody.

Learned people know how far harsh words will affect others. They give everyman their ears but not their voice. Knowing its vicious potency, they will never speak injuriously on others. They will maintain their calmness and gentleness.

Comparable are the couplets of Tirukkural-129 and 305.

காவாது, ஒருவன் தன் வாய் திறந்து சொல்லும் சொல்
ஓவாதே தம்மைச் சுடுதலால், ஓவாதே
ஆய்ந்து அமைந்த கேள்வி அறிவுடையார், எஞ் ஞான்றும்,
காய்ந்து அமைந்த சொல்லார், கறுத்து.

64. Unequals in front of us utter uncultured words but
 Great men never feel and get infuriated whereas
 The low-bred cogitate about and repeat them aloud
 Dashed against pillars and jump hither and thither.

The gist of this stanza is that those who eliminate anger are the great men of high caliber and those who poignantly hold it in mind and get extremely agitated and perturbed are of low caliber.

நேர்த்து, நிகர் அல்லார் நீர் அல்ல சொல்லியக்கால்,
வேர்த்து வெகுளார், விழுமியோர்; ஓர்த்து அதனை,
உள்ளத்தான் உள்ளி, உரைத்து, உராய், ஊர் கேட்ப,
துள்ளி, தூண் முட்டுமாம், கீழ்.

65. Energetic youth's self control is real control
    Incomeless person's liberality is actual munificence
    Patience of an ascetic despite his fury and strength
    In controlling vindictiveness is a towering toleration.

There is no wonder if an old man is in self restraint. He cannot but be so due to his old age. But if a virile youth does so, it is an admirable self-control. So also the liberality of a poor man and the toleration of an ascetic in curbing vindictiveness. Practically speaking, these are difficult prepositions but in performing them lies their achievement.

> இளையான் அடக்கம் அடக்கம்; கிளை பொருள்
> இல்லான் கொடையே கொடைப் பயன்; எல்லாம்
> ஒறுக்கும் மதுகை உரனுடையாளன்
> பொறுக்கும் பொறையே பொறை.

66. Harsh words darted by bad men as stones pelted at,
    Wise men publicly bear and wipe them out
    Because of their preventive nobility as cobra
    Restrain its hood when charmed ashes thrown at it.

Wise men bear harsh words of worthless persons as cobras contain their fury at the spell of a magic. Not known whether a cobra is controllable by magic spell or charmed ashes. May be apocryphal. Restraint and toleration even on provocation are said to be the appreciable qualities maintained by wisemen and ascetics. Those are the noble qualities which they observe in ascetism.

> கல் எறிந்தன்ன கயவர் வாய் இன்னாச் சொல்
> எல்லாரும் காணப் பொறுத்து, உய்ப்பர்-ஒல்லை,
> இடு நீற்றால் பை அவிந்த நாகம்போல், தம்தம்
> குடிமையான் வாதிக்கப்பட்டு.

67. Wisemen wouldn't say it inability if hold
    No enmity against those who are inimical;
    Hence if such unwise inflict harm impatiently on us
    Desirable it is not to do the same against them.

Gist of this poem is that we should not do any harm even to those who deliberately offend and harm us. Such extra-ordinary patience is cowardliness for the kshatriya clan but a noble quality for asceties. *Kshatriyas* are the royal group in the four – fold classification known as *varnashrama* in Indian society.

> மாற்றாராய் நின்று, தம் மாறு ஏற்பார்க்கு ஏலாமை,
> 'ஆற்றாமை' என்னார், அறிவுடையார்; ஆற்றாமை
> நேர்ந்து, இன்னா மற்று அவர் செய்தக்கால், தாம் அவரைப்
> பேர்த்து இன்னா செய்யாமை நன்று.

68. Wrath of petty - men, even after a long time
    Will continue to be alive and go on increasing;
    But of dignified person's will be like the heat
    Getting itself cooled after the water is boiled.

Lowbred people will harbor their enmity and continue to hold it for a long time. But reverential, dignified and gentle persons will not only not harbouring their wrath but forget it for ever. Vide stanza 23 of *Vakkundam,* an ethical work in Tamil.

> நெடுங் காலம் ஓடினும், நீசர் வெகுளி
> கெடும் காலம் இன்றிப் பரக்கும்; அடும் காலை
> நீர் கொண்ட வெப்பம்போல் தானே தணியுமே
> சீர் கொண்ட சான்றோர் சினம்.

69. Unmindful of benefits done, one causes
    Evils in plenty; doing good again to that offender
    Instead of planning harm to him
    Is to be found among those born of dignified family.

Those born of dignified families will continue to extend benefits even if the beneficiary does harm, forgetting the help done to him earlier. Sense of gratitude is indirectly emphasized here.

> உபகாரம் செய்ததனை ஓராதே, தங்கண்
> அபகாரம் ஆற்றச் செயினும், உபகாரம்
> தாம் செய்வது அல்லாலல், தவற்றினால் தீங்கு ஊக்கல்
> வான் தோய் குடிப் பிறந்தார்க்கு இல்.

70. Seeing an angry dog pounced on and bitten
    Nobody here retaliated and bitten it back;
    So when lowbred speak ill and a bad language,
    Will the dignified ever be speaking ill against them?

No great man will ever stoop to the level of using abusive language if somebody has insulted and spoken vicious language against him. *Give the devil its due* may be applicable elsewhere but not in the domain of highly respectable and dignified persons.

> கூர்த்து நாய் கௌவிக் கொளக் கண்டும், தம் வாயால்
> பேர்த்து நாய் கௌவினார் ஈங்கு இல்லை; நீர்த்து அன்றிக்
> கீழ்மக்கள் கீழ் ஆய சொல்லியக்கால், சொல்பவோ,
> மேன்மக்கள் தம் வாயால் மீட்டு?

Division - II - Family Life

Chapter 8 - Sense of toleration
***

Sense of toleration is one of the qualities to be practised in family life in addition to the avoidance of fury and emotion.

71. Lord of a cool hilly nation of garland-like cascade!
    Do not mingle with and talk to the unwise;
    Lest he would distort what you said and hence
    Keep you away from him gradually.

If persons of lower caliber distort your talk, avoid their company. Your counseling, if any may even be distorted by them and hence desirable it is to disconnect their contact slowly but steadily. Counselling the fool is neither conducive nor desirable.

கோதை அருவிக் குளிர் வரை நல் நாட!
பேதையோடு யாதும் உரையற்க! பேதை,
உரைக்கின், சிதைந்து உரைக்கும்; ஒல்லும் வகையால்,
வழுக்கிக் கழிதலே நன்று.

72. If unequals speak odd and uncultured,
    Virtuous forbear those words and if not
    The intolerance of wise men may be deemed
    Despicable and unappreciable by worldly elders.

It is fitting in with the status of good people to tolerate insulting words of low-bred persons. Tit for tat wouldn't be fair. Otherwise the intolerance will be unappreciable by great men. Sweet words of inimical persons may be harmful. Even harsh words of noble persons will bring in benevolence.

நேர் அல்லார் நீர் அல்ல சொல்லியக்கால், மற்று அது
தாரித்திருத்தல் தகுதி; மற்று ஒரும்
புகழ்மையாக் கொள்ளாது, பொங்கு நீர் ஞாலம்
சமழ்மையாக் கொண்டுவிடும்.

73. O coastal chieftain of flowers abound with
    humming bees!
    If only we have loving friends of cordiality
    Harsh words of those friends wouldn't be harmful
    But the sweet words of unfriendly men would do.

Harsh words of genuinely affectionate friends would be benevolent but even the loving words of inimical persons would be harmful. Hence tolerating the strong words of loving elders is always desirable.

காதலார் சொல்லும் கடுஞ் சொல், உவந்து உரைக்கும்
ஏதிலார் இன் சொலின் தீது ஆமோ-போது எலாம்
மாதர் வண்டு ஆர்க்கும் மலி கடல் தண் சேர்ப்ப!
ஆவது அறிவார்ப் பெறின்?

74. Humbly knowledgeable and fearful of sins
    Perform duties pleasantly to the world and these
    Men who are fearful of those to be feared in life
    Never encounter any suffering at all.

Those who could discriminate good things from bad and are fearful for those to be feared and perform benevolent deeds will lead a happy and pleasant life and never encounter any misery at all. This poem has an echo of Kural II-5-8.

அறிவது அறிந்து, அடங்கி, அஞ்சுவது அஞ்சி,
உறுவது உலகு உவப்பச் செய்து, பெறுவதனால்
இன்புற்று வாழும் இயல்புடையார், எஞ் ஞான்றும்,
துன்புற்று வாழ்தல் அரிது.

75. Of two men who are friendly sans divisiveness
    If one is found to be of gross misconduct,
    Bear with it till a limit and if he is unbearable
    Keep him at a distance without scandalizing.

Two persons have been close friends for a long time. But if one of the two is found to be very bad in behavior, let the other one tolerate it to a bearable level and if other one goes unbearably bad, leave him off without openly speaking ill of his misbehavior.

> வேற்றுமை இன்றிக் கலந்து, இருவர் நட்டக்கால்,
> தேற்றா ஒழுக்கம் ஒருவன்கண் உண்டாயின்,
> ஆற்றும் துணையும் பொறுக்க! பொறான் ஆயின்
> தூற்றாதே, தூர விடல்!

76. Even if close friends do harm, deem it good
    Blame yourself for its sequences but to
    Give up those close friends, O! Lord
    Of wild jungles! Even animals wouldn't do.

Whatever may be the reasons, close friends should not be disconnected. One should tolerate even if they commit harm to you. This is the noblest form of camaraderie.

> 'இன்னா செயினும், இனிய ஒழிக! என்று,
> தன்னையே தான் நோவின் அல்லது, துன்னிக்
> கலந்தாரைக் கைவிடுதல்-கானக நாட!
> விலங்கிற்கும் விள்ளல் அரிது!

77. Holding exalted amity with great people
    Is because of their tolerance of our gross follies;
    O! lord of rattling falls and lofty hills !
    Friends will never be rare for those great men.

A lot of friends will be there for those great men of tolerance and humility. Even when we knowingly or unknowingly commit blunders, they have the patience to withstand them.

பெரியார் பெரு நட்புக் கோடல், தாம் செய்த
அரிய பொறுப்ப என்று அன்றோ? அரியரோ
ஒல்லென் அருவி உயர் வரை நல் நாட!
நல்ல செய்வார்க்குத் தமர்?

78. Even if hunger is so acute to emaciate you
Don't speak of it to discourteous persons;
Those who aren't bold to renounce in life
May convey to those who could eliminate their
                                  indigence.

Obviously this stanza is addressed to those who are inclined to lead a life of renunciation. Even under extreme poverty, they should not speak of it to men of impropriety. But only to those who could help eliminating their poverty.

வற்றி, மற்று ஆற்றப் பசிப்பினும், பண்பு இலார்க்கு
அற்றம் அறிய உரையற்க! அற்றம்
மறைக்கும் துணையார்க்கு உரைப்பவே, தம்மைத்
துறக்கும் துணிவு இலாதார்.

79. Even if stigma comes along with happiness
You are inclined of the same and if that happiness
Continues to exist with you, O! Lord of cascades !
Better it is not to indulge in reproachful actions.

Even when mundane happiness is stigmatized, average men and women may be inclined to enjoy it. In case of that questionable happiness continues to exist because of their efforts, one should behave in right direction without getting his actions condemned.

இன்பம் பயந்தாங்கு இழிவு தலைவரினும்,
இன்பத்தின் பக்கம் இருந்தைக்க! இன்பம்
ஒழியாமை கண்டாலும்-ஓங்கு அருவி நாட!
பழி ஆகா ஆறே தலை.

80. Even on your ruin, don't think of ruining the great;
In becoming thin and lean, don't eat from improper men,
Even if you get the whole earth under the canopy of sky
Do not utter any word blended with lies.

When one suffers in poverty, he should not think of getting resource by ruining others and shouldn't think of eating from the hands of low-level persons. Never should he utter a word of lie even if the whole world is given to him.

தான் கெடினும், தக்கார் கேடு எண்ணற்க! தன் உடம்பின்
ஊன் கெடினும், உண்ணார் கைத்து உண்ணற்க! வான் கவிந்த
வையகம் எல்லாம் பெறினும், உரையற்க,
பொய்யோடு இடை மிடைந்த சொல்!

Chapter 9 - Yearning not others wives
***

Love is normal but lust in abnormal. Controlling the lust is a great virtue. Senses will arouse the sexual passion. But one should tolerate this physiological nuisance. That is why this chapter follows the counselling of toleration.

81. Fear is great, paltry its joy and if deeply
    Think, royal penalty of death besides an action
    Evil to lead to hell and if you shy of these
    Shameful actions, desire not others wives.

This is like a mild warning to those who covet the wife of another person. Fear of being assaulted by de jure husband, a carnal joy that is short-lived, a likely punishment of even death by the ruler of the country and an eternal punishment of hell after death will be the resultant effect of adultery. Anyone who is shy of these possible punishments, should desist himself from desiring the wives of others.

> அச்சம் பெரிதால்; அதற்கு இன்பம் சிற்றளவால்;
> நிச்சம் நினையுங்கால் கோக் கொலையால்; நிச்சலும்
> கும்பிக்கே கூர்த்த வினையால்;-பிறன் தாரம்
> நம்பற்க, நாண் உடையார்!

82. Virtue, fame, intimacy and glory would
    Never associate if one covets another's wife;
    But still on those who do desire other's wife
    Enmity, blame, sin and fear would attach them
                                                    with.

Desiring of another man's wife is uncharitable. It won't earn the respect of others. Such action would incur the displeasure of one and all. Lust is one of the five notorious sins. Hence this clandestine activity of enjoying the trivial pleasure with a neighbour's wife is all the more condemned here. This stanza is comparable to Kural No.146.

> அறம், புகழ், கேண்மை, பெருமை இந் நான்கும்
> பிறன் தாரம் நச்சுவார்ச் சேரா; பிறன் தாரம்
> நச்சுவார்ச் சேரும், பகை, பழி, பாவம் என்று
> அச்சத்தோடு இந் நாற் பொருள்.

83. Fear at entry and so too during exit
    Fear in enjoying her and so too to keep its secrecy
    So a fear for ever in this clandestine role –
    Who else will be fearless to go to another's wife?

Nothing but fear alone would preoccupy the mind of a person who indulges in illegitimate intimacy with the wife of another person. This stanza implies therefore that any sensitive person would be fearfully unwilling to concubinage.

> புக்க இடத்து அச்சம்; போதரும் போது அச்சம்;
> துய்க்கும் இடத்து அச்சம்; தோன்றாமைக் காப்பு அச்சம்;
> எக் காலும் அச்சம் தருமால்; எவன்கொலோ,
> உட்கான், பிறன் இல் புகல்?

84. If known, a reproach to lineage and if caught
    Legs get cut off and a fear when you do it!
    Hellish penalty will you get; O misbehaved!
    Moreover, how much have got in immoral pleasure?

This is purported to have been addressed to an adulterous person. Because of his immorality, his family will get a bad name. It is curious to know that kings as a penalty seem to have cut off a person's leg in those days for a proven case of immorality. There had been a belief that men of depraved behavior will go to hell. In spite of all these hurdles and setbacks, what pleasure an immoral person can have? The poem is posing this question and silently warns a person to behave properly without any sexual stigma in his worldly life.

> காணின், குடிப் பழி ஆம்; கையுறின், கால் குறையும்;
> ஆண் இன்மை செய்யுங்கால், அச்சம் ஆம்; நீள் நிரயத்
> துன்பம் பயக்குமால்; துச்சாரி! நீ கண்ட
> இன்பம், எனக்கு, எனைத்தால்? கூறு.

85. Devoid of morality with persons of low caliber
    To caress shoulders of globular breasted woman
    By forceful entry into other's house are those
    Who struggle for existence as eunuchs in this life.

This stanza is on a belief that those who are eunuchs and impotent in this temporal world are those who in their previous birth violently intruded into the houses of others to enjoy illegitimate intimacy with women. Hence it is the presumption of the poet that the enunch-hood is a providential punishment.

> செம்மை ஒன்று இன்றி, சிறியார் இனத்தர் ஆய்,
> கொம்மை வரி முலையாள் தோள் மரீஇ, உம்மை,
> வலியால் பிறர் மனைமேல் சென்றாரே-இம்மை,
> அலி ஆகி, ஆடி உண்பார்.

86. On a date chosen, fixed and with notice to public
    Marriage held at a safe home after tom-toming;
    Despite living with such a loving and gentle wife,
    Why should anyone be lustful for anothers's wife?

One can have a connubial pleasure, with his wife on the basis of conjugal rights. When this possibility is at home, why should anyone be after a highly objectionable and contemptible behavior? If so, one may critically question whether an aged bachelor who has remained alone at home is at liberty to advance towards the wife of another? The very aim of this decad under

Yearning not another's wife' is to object such illegitimate relationship and not to advocate it at all.

> பல்லார் அறியப் பறை அறைந்து, நாள் கேட்டு,
> கல்யாணம் செய்து, கடி புக்க மெல் இயல்.
> காதல் மனையாளும் இல்லாளா, என், ஒருவன்
> ஏதில் மனையாளை நோக்கு?

87. Amidst the gossip of others and kin's fearful regret
    Sensuous joy of an incredulous and perfidious person
    In having enjoyed a friend's wife
    Is like licking a glossy hood of a deadly snake.

Clandestine intimacy with a friend's wife is not only treacherous but it gives room for a widespread gossip among the neighbours. Such a carnal pleasure and sensuous rapture are as dangerous as that of kissing the glossy hood of a snake.

> அம்பல் அயல் எடுப்ப, அஞ்சித் தமர் பரீஇ,
> வம்பலன் பெண் மரீஇ, மைந்துற்று, நம்பும்
> நிலைமை இல் நெஞ்சத்தான் துப்புரவு-பாம்பின்
> தலை நக்கியன்னது உடைத்து.

88. The disease of lust is so cruel among men of wisdom'
    Won't increase, never comes out and cling on to many
    Shyness of likely to be known to others would
    Keep him unexpressive but get it cooled within!

Even among men of wisdom, lust will create an excitement. But because of their status, the sense of lust-would neither increase, nor appears explicit in them. A fear will be lingering within whether it will be known to others. However, the sense of lust will lie dormant among them but by stages, it will get cooled.

பரவா, வெளிப்படா, பல்லோர்கண் தங்கா,
உரவோர்கண் காம நோய், ஓஒ கொடிதே!
விரவாருள் நாணுப்படல் அஞ்சி, யாதும்
உரையாது, உள் ஆறிவிடும்.

89. Blaze, arrow and sparkling rays of the fiery sun
    Even though very hot are just external, but
    Lust of women worries and burns us internally
    And hence more feared of than all these.

Fire arrow and rays of the sun are externally painful. But lust is internally miserable and hence to be avoided. Even though the stanza distinctly enumerates the characteristic feature of lust, the implication is that no one should be enamoured of the wife of others.

அம்பும், அழலும், அவிர் கதிர் ஞாயிறும்,
வெம்பிச் சுடினும், புறம் சுடும்; வெம்பிக்
கவற்றி மனத்தைச் சுடுதலால், காமம்
அவற்றினும் அஞ்சப்படும்.

90. One can survive blazing fire that has
    Arisen in hamlet by plunging into a pond;
    But lust would burn even in dipping into water
    And so too even when hiding in cavernous mount.

If a person is engulfed by fire he can escape from it by plunging into a pond. But if he is controlled by lust, he could escape neither by a pond nor by climbing on a hillock. It is suggested therefore that no man should give room for lust. For any man or woman, love is natural and normal. But lust is abnormal and hence it is contemptible.

ஊருள் எழுந்த உரு கெழு செந் தீக்கு
நீருள் குளித்தும் உயல் ஆகும்; நீருள்
குளிப்பினும், காமம் சுடுமே; குன்று ஏறி
ஒளிப்பினும், காமம் சுடும்.

☙ ♦ ❖ ♦ ❧

Chapter 10 - Donation
***

91. To those persons who help the indigent poor
    With little or nothing but to the extent possible
    Happily as if resourceful and with manners gentle,
    The doors of heaven aren't kept locked.

The idea behind this is that when poor persons approach for help even when the donor is not that must rich as he had been, he should try to help as much as possible and to him the doors of heaven will be kept open. Despite one's own ups and downs, one must be liberal in helping others. This generosity will lead him to paradise.

> இல்லா இடத்தும், இயைந்த அளவினால்
> உள்ள இடம்போல் பெரிது உவந்து, மெல்லக்
> கொடையொடு பட்ட குணனுடை மாந்தர்க்கு
> அடையாவாம், ஆண்டைக் கதவு.

92. Day of demise, hateful old age confront you
    Also weakening sickness and so let there be
    No boasting of your wealth, neither enamoring of it
    Nor suppressing of it but enjoy sharing it with
                                              others.

Seems to have been addressed to the miserly house holders as a forewarning that they should be charitable and ethical. With the wealth they have, they should be liberal and transparent in their lifestyle, because the day of demise may come at any time.

> முன்னரே, சாம் நாள், முனிதக்க மூப்பு, உள;
> பின்னரும் பீடு அழிக்கும் நோய் உள; கொன்னே
> பரவன்மின்; பற்றன்மின்; பாத்து உண்மின்; யாதும்
> கரவன்மின், கைத்துண்டாம் போழ்து.

93. You don't wipe off the misery of help - seekers;
　　　Wealth, if destined, is bound to grow even if
　　　　　　　　　　　　　　　　　　　spent lavishly
　　　If not, even if hold tightly, it wont remain and
　　　It wouldn't be with you, when the destiny dries
　　　　　　　　　　　　　　　　　　　　　　　off.

Key note of the passage is that if destiny favours, one's own wealth would multiply if not, it would vanish and depart. Wealth is on the diktat of destiny. Neither does it increase when hold up tightly nor does it decrease if one spends lavishly. Hence be of assistance and liberal to others.

> நடுக்குற்றுத் தற் சேர்ந்தார் துன்பம் துடையார்;
> கொடுத்துத் தான் துய்ப்பினும், ஈண்டுங்கால் ஈண்டும்;
> மிடுக்கு உற்றுப் பற்றினும், நில்லாது செல்வம்,
> விடுக்கும் வினை உலந்தக்கால்.

94. Eat daily after feeding those who are indigent ;
　　　Even a minuscule of it as much as possible or else
　　　Beggars who have no hearth of their own in the
　　　　　　　　　　　　　　　　　　　　　　world
　　　Of oceans around would curse you as a miser.

This counselling to the houseolders reiterate that they should part with, even a fingerful of food from what they eat; otherwise, beggars who wander about would go on cursing that you are a beggarly miser. The syntax of the Tamil original gives room for a definition that those who are mendicants in this birth were, in their previous birth, stingy misers. Hence they wander about presently. So, be liberal and generous so that you can escape from being born as a beggar in the next birth.

> இம்மி அரிசித் துணையானும், வைகலும்,
> நும்மில் இயைவ கொடுத்து உண்மின்;-நும்மைக்
> கொடாஅதவர் என்பர், குண்டு நீர் வையத்து
> அடாஅ அடுப்பினவர்.

95. Being mindful of terrestrial and celestial life
 One should generous be in offering donations; If
 Impossible due to one's poverty, himself not
 Begging will be doubly better than donations.

Keynote of the poem is to prevent people from begging. It's a curse if people go on wandering in the streets for begging. Unavoidably if somebody does it, a householder may offer something possible. If not, he in his level shouldn't go down to a level of beggary on any account.

> மறுமையும் இம்மையும் நோக்கி, ஒருவற்கு
> உறுமாறு இயைவ கொடுத்தல்! வறுமையால்
> ஈதல் இசையாதுளெனினும், இரவாமை
> ஈதல் இரட்டி உறும்.

96. Those who live an adorable life are like palm trees
 That have a circular platform to enable it to be
 enjoyed;
 Those wealthy but never shares even little to others
 Are like male species of palm tree that stands
 adrift in a graveyard.

The female species of palm trees will be protected in villages and taken care for the sake of their natural product such as their fruits, fronds and their stems. This is a part of natural scenery in rural areas. Those who are misers in not doing anything benevolent to others are compared to the unproductive male species of palm trees.

> நடு ஊருள் வேதிகை சுற்றுக்கோள் புக்க
> படு பனை அன்னர், பலர் நச்ச வாழ்வார்;
> குடி கொழுத்தக்கண்ணும், கொடுத்து உண்ணா மாக்கள்
> இடுகாட்டுள் ஏற்றைப் பனை.

97. Ye, the owner of a coastal area where the smell of fishes
Are replaced by the fragrance of *punnai* flowers;
How would the world survive, if seasonal rains
Fail and if wealthy people are not charitable.

Implication is that those who are rich have to be humanistic and charitable. Substance of this poem is like an appeal to wealthy people to be generous and helpful to the poor and the needy.

பெயற்பால் மழை பெய்யாக்கண்ணும், உலகம்
செயற்பால செய்யாவிடினும்,-கயல் புலால்
புன்னை கடியும் பொரு கடல் தண் சேர்ப்ப!
என்னை உலகு உய்யும் ஆறு?

98. Ye, the owner of cool coastal area!
Duty of a male is to extend help sans setting aside
The hands that beg but to offer it to those
Who could repay is analogous to a virtual debt.

Unmindful of whether a person is solvent or not, one should provide all kinds of help, but extending an aid only to those who are capable of returning it will be deemed to be a virtual debt.

ஏற்ற கை, மாற்றாமை, என்னானும் தாம் வரையாது,
ஆற்றதார்க்கு ஈவது ஆம் ஆண் கடன்; ஆற்றின்,
மலி கடல் தண் சேர்ப்ப!-மாறு ஈவார்க்கு ஈதல்
பொலி கடன் என்னும் பெயர்த்து.

99. Neither you should say nay nor give little to those
Who beg but extend charity to everybody; This
Will complete your benevolence slowly but steadily
As the alms vessel of a monk is filled at every door step.

The act of charity is emphasized in this stanza also. One should do the help without excusing himself. This benevolent action on his part will make him eligible to the world celestial.

இறப்பச் சிறிது என்னாது, இல் என்னாது, என்றும்,
அறப்பயன் யார் மாட்டும் செய்க! முறைப் புதவின்
ஐயம் புகூஉம் தவசி கடிஞைபோல்,
பைய நிறைத்து விடும்.

100. Sound of a drum can be heard at tenth mile
Ferocious thunder may even be heard at fortieth mile
But the word of the elders that 'he donated hugely
Will be heard in the three words of the universe.

May appear to be a hyperbolic statement but it is to speak highly of the generosity of the donors. The term *'Katham'* in the original is roughly estimated to be equal to ten miles or sixteen kilometers of modern days. The three worlds are - Nether world, terrestrial World and the Celestial World.

கடிப்பு இடு கண் முரசம் காதத்தோர் கேட்பர்;
இடித்து முழங்கியது ஓர் யோசனையோர் கேட்பர்;
அடுக்கிய மூஉலகும் கேட்குமே, சான்றோர்
கொடுத்தார் எனப்படும் சொல்.

ಛ ♦ ❖ ♦ ಬಾ

Chapter 11- Activities done in previous births
***

Traditional belief is what has been done in previous birth will consequently bring in proportional benefit or otherwise in the present life. Those who did good and benevolent activities in their previous birth will have their life pleasant in the present life and those who were of bad actions and ill – reputed will endure their worldly life unpleasantly. This is the major theme and keynote of the following ten stanzas. As these are closely related to one's own generosity or otherwise, it is relevantly placed next to the chapter on the quality of giving.

101. Even when led into a herd of Cows, the Calf
     Is capable of reaching its mother and so also
     The actions of previous birth to reach presently
     And hold a person who did them then.

The actions and deeds of a man in his previous birth catch hold of him presently and put him into either a pleasant or unpleasant experience, depending upon what he had done then. What is implied therefore is that men should think positively and do benevolent actions in worldly life.

> பல் ஆவுள் உய்த்துவிடினும், குழக் கன்று
> வல்லது ஆம், தாய் நாடிக் கோடலை; தொல்லைப்
> பழவினையும் அன்ன தகைத்தே, தற் செய்த
> கிழவனை நாடிக் கொளற்கு.

102. Despite aware the image, youth, honour wealth
                                                 aren't
     One and the same with everybody, a person
     Who doesn't do anything good in this life
     Will simply exist, survive and extinguish.

This poem implies, therefore that a man should think in terms of doing good to others. If not adequately now, in the next birth, certainly he would enjoy a proportionate harm and happiness only in life. The object of one's own life must be to learn, earn and do good to others. If not, he will simply lead a meaningless life and die unwept unhonoured and unsung.

> உருவும், இளமையும், ஒண் பொருளும், உட்கும்,
> ஒரு வழி நில்லாமை கண்டும், ஒரு வழி
> ஒன்றேயும் இல்லாதான் வாழ்க்கை உடம்பு இட்டு
> நின்று வீழ்ந் தக்கது உடைத்து.

103. None doesn't like rich, resourceful life
    But measured are the ways of life in proportion
    To what they did ere as none has shaped
    Vilaankai into globular nor has blackened *kalaankai*

The tropical fruits - *Vilaankai and Kalaankai* are round in shape and black in colour respectively. None has made them either into a shape or into a colour. Similarly if a man is fabulously rich, it is because of his benevolent deeds in his previous birth. This implies that men should focus their attention to do good deeds and benevolent actions in the present life.

> வளம் பட வேண்டாதார் யார்? யாரும் இல்லை;
> அளந்தன போகம், அவர் அவர் ஆற்றால்;
> விளங்காய் திரட்டினார் இல்லை; களங் கனியைக்
> கார் எனச் செய்தாரும் இல்.

104. If it's drought, nobody could bring rains
    If rains pour excessively, nobody could arrest
    So do removal of sufferings that even saints can't
    And arrival of blessings too in life can't be
                                                        prevented.

So are the resultant effects of what one does in his previous birth. These cannot be shaped or reshaped by man's efforts.

Strenuous human efforts are of no use according to this stanza. References to the unconquerable forces of Nature, be a drought or deluge are quite convincing. Can these be straight away applied to the happiness or suffering of a man in his current life? Can't a suffering person work hard and remove the hurdles and be happy? These are the thought provoking queries that come to our mind when we analyse the poem.

> உறற்பால நீக்கல் உறுவர்க்கும் ஆகா;
> பெறற்பால் அனையவும் அன்ன ஆம்;-மாரி
> வறப்பின், தருவாரும் இல்லை; அதனைச்
> சிறப்பின், தணிப்பாரும் இல்.

105. From a level of pleni potentiary a few declined
    And lead a graceless life as puny as a small grain;
    What else the reason to analyse other than what
    Evil deeds they committed in their previous birth?

Even those who led a luxurious life with all reputation, at one stage in life come down to endure a graceless life of penury. The reason behind this is what evil deed they committed in their previous birth has reflected in their present downfall. But how to explain their affluence and fame in their early life? That must be due to their benevolent activities partially done by them in their previous birth.

> தினைத் துணையர் ஆகி, தம் தேசு உள் அடக்கி,
> பனைத் துணையார் வைகலும் பாடு அழிந்து வாழ்வர்;
> நினைப்பக் கிடந்தது எவன் உண்டாம், மேலை
> வினைப்பயன் அல்லால், பிற?

106. Know thou the reason for early demise of veterans
    And longer life of illiterate idiots in the world?
    Death greatly enamoured of acquiring geniuses
    Neglecting the hollow men of illiteracy behind.

Here the poet's real intention is to emphasise that either the longevity of life among the illiterates or the short duration of geniuses is on the basis of what deeds they have done in their previous birth. But actually his reference to the God of Death and his passion to snatch away the life of versatile geniuses is to highlight the excellence of knowledge and intelligence.

பல் ஆன்ற கேள்விப் பயன் உணர்வார் வீயவும்,
கல்லாதார் வாழ்வது அறிதிரேல், கல்லாதார்
சேதனம் என்னும் அச் சேறு அகத்து இன்மையால்
கோது என்று கொள்ளாதாம், கூற்று.

107. Ye the owner of a coastal region where the swans
 Tore the flowers of *adambam* on the wavy line of
 sea-shores,
 Those poverty - stricken wait at the gates of rich
 Is because of evil that they did in previous birth.

Few men suffer from acute poverty. This is a consequence of actions and deeds that they performed in their earlier birth. Had they benevolently behaved, they would not suffer now. The present wretched life is a retribution for what they did in those days of the past.

இடும்பை கூர் நெஞ்சத்தார் எல்லாரும் காண,
நெடுங் கடை நின்று உழல்வது எல்லாம்,-அடும்பம்பூ
அன்னம் கிழிக்கும் அலை கடல் தண் சேர்ப்ப!
முன்னை வினை ஆய்விடும்.

108. Ye, the owner of a coastal region where the
 Blowing wind disseminate the honey of *neithal*
 Not ignorant at all but men are aware of all known;
 But men's evil attitude is due to former birth.

Talented and knowledgeable they are; but they too do revengeful activities. This is because of their vulnerable actions in their earlier birth; they need a better counsel.

அறியாரும் அல்லர்; அறிவது அறிந்தும்,
பழியோடு பட்டவை செய்தல்,-வளி ஓடி
நெய்தல் நறவு உயிர்க்கும் நீள் கடல் தண் சேர்ப்ப!
செய்த வினையான் வரும்.

109. Everybody in the world bordered by oceans
Wishes not any misery but desire merry;
Whether you desire it or not, pleasure
And pain that come of their own accord, leave you not

The substance of the poem is that happiness and misery that occur in our terrestrial life is not according to our own wishes or otherwise but as per the actions we performed in earlier birth. In other words, merriness and sorrow come of their own accord and we are simply at the receiving end.

ஈண்டு நீர் வையத்துள், எல்லாரும், எத்துணையும்
வேண்டார்மன், தீய; விழைபயன், நல்லவை;
வேண்டினும், வேண்டாவிடினும், உறற்பால
தீண்டாவிடுதல் அரிது.

110. Destiny, congenitally ordained in man
Neither decrease nor increase nor dislocate
Nor will it be supportive but will go on in its way
So why should a man be miserable of it in last
                                                                    days?

The destiny is due to a man's previous birth and it is ordained on him. So what is congenitally destined on a man will have its effect on him, however much he tries to influence it and bring it in his own way. What the poem asserts is that destiny is an invincible force and it is pre-ordained on every individual. Note that this poem is in contradistinction to the substance of Kural-620. *Those who labour intensively will push destiny behind their back.*

சிறுகா, பெருகா, முறை பிறழ்ந்து வாரா,
உறு காலத்து ஊற்று ஆகா, ஆம் இடத்தே ஆகும்,
சிறுகாலைப் பட்ட பொறியும்; அதனால்,
இறுகாலத்து, என்னை பரிவு?

Chapter 12 - Essence of Truth
***

Following ten stanzas insist on the importance of truth, wealth, humbleness, nobility and self-respect.

111. Lady of bangles ! Not an offence but worldly
To say No when you truly cannot help a needy; but
After a delay to say a lie that you cannot by killing
Their hopes an offence worse than ingratitude.

What the stanza outlines is that those who say that they are actually not able to help the poor are honest but others who after giving certain hopes and tell a lie that they are unable to, even when they are rich and resourceful is not only dishonest but may even be deemed criminal . An allied proverb for honest persons is. *Be slow to promise but quick to perform.*

> இசையா ஒரு பொருள் இல் என்றல், யார்க்கும்
> வசை அன்று; வையத்து இயற்கை; நசை அழுங்க
> நின்று ஓடிப் பொய்த்தல்,-நிரைதொடீஇ! செய்ந்நன்றி
> கொன்றாரின் குற்றம் உடைத்து.

112. Dignified and undignified behave proportionately
Without any mitigation of their true quality
As sugar will never be bitter whoever taste it
But neem is bitter even if semi-divines taste it.

Sugar will be tasty whoever consumes it. Similarly neem will be bitter even if semi divine beings taste it. So also, virtuous people of dignified behavior will certainly reveal their good qualities wherever they mingle. But undignified and offensive characters will display their bad qualities whenever they move about. Hence avoid the company of questionable persons.

தக்காரும் தக்கவர் அல்லாரும், தம் நீர்மை
எக்காலும் குன்றல் இலர் ஆவர்;-அக்காரம்
யாவரே தின்னினும் கையாதாம்; கைக்குமாம்,
தேவரே தின்னினும், வேம்பு.

113. Ye, ruler of a hilly country. For luxurious richman,
Kindred will be more than even the stars of bluish sky;
When the richman endures heavy trouble, few alone
Would say they are closely related and offer him help.

Customary habit of the world is that around fabulously rich men, many will easily come around and get associated. If those rich men fell on evil days and suffer, few alone would come forward to give them a helping hand.

What is obliquely conveyed here is the importance of managing one's own wealth. Mismanagement of wealth will render him a lot of problems and suffering.

கால் ஆடு போழ்தில், கழி கிளைஞர், வானத்து
மேல் ஆடும் மீனின் பலர் ஆவர்; ஏலா
இடர் ஒருவர் உற்றக்கால்,-ஈர்ங் குன்ற நாட!
'தொடர்பு உடையேம் என்பார் சிலர்'.

114. Of charity, wealth and love of this spotless world
Acquiring the middle will lead to do the other two;
Not the middle, render him the misery
As much as that of getting boiled in an oven.

Those who possess wealth in the world will be able to acquire love and extend charity to others. Those who do not possess it will undergo incalculable suffering and agony in life.

வடு இலா வையத்து, மன்னிய மூன்றில்,
நடுவணது எய்த, இரு தலையும் எய்தும்;
நடுவணது எய்தாதான் எய்தும், உலைப் பெய்து,
அடுவது போலும் துயர்.

115. If it's a calf of high breed cow, it is easily sold,even
If unlettered, a rich man's word is surely respected;
But word of the poor won't be heard and be heeded
As a plough can't go deeper into a less-moistured soil.

The words of a rich man will be heard even if he is illiterate and unwise. Even though a poor man is honest and knowledgeable, his words and his counseling will not be heard. Nobody will respect him. In other words, everybody will despise the poor but praise the rich. This practical aspect of the world is what the stanza explains.

> நல் ஆவின் கன்றுஆயின், நாகும் விலை பெறூஉம்;
> கல்லாரே ஆயினும், செல்வர் வாய்ச் சொல் செல்லும்.
> புல் ஈரப் போழ்தின் உழவேபோல் மீது ஆடி,
> செல்லாவாம், நல்கூர்ந்தார் சொல்.

116. Ye, the wide-eyed damsel! Even if deeply learnt
A lot of treatises, arrogant will never be humble; as
Wild *suraikkai* never get rid of its bitterness even
If cooked with salt, ghee, milk, curd and asafoetida

In-built bitter taste of *Suraikkai* will never go even if delicious ingredients such as ghee, milk and curd and potential spices such as salt and asafoetida are added into it when cooking. Similarly the congenital arrogance of a man cannot be deprived of him even if he has learnt a lot of philosophical treatises.

> இடம் பட மெய்ஞ்ஞானம் கற்பினும் என்றும்,
> அடங்காதார் என்றும் அடங்கார்;-தடங் கண்ணாய்!
> உப்பொடு நெய், பால், தயிர், காயம், பெய்து அடினும்,
> கைப்பு அறா, பேய்ச் சுரையின் காய்.

117. Ye, reputed lord of the coast of florid *punnai* groves!
Those who wantonly insult us have to be insulted.
Even earlier because what else to be got from them?
Joys and sorrows are bound to come anyway in life.

In spite of earlier familiarity, if anybody behaves neglectingly or insultingly, get rid of such contact. Not that there had been anything useful because of him nor does it cause, any evil if that familiarity is gotten rid of. Self – respect and one's own dignity are more important in a man's life. He must maintain them at any rate.

> தம்மை இகழ்வாரைத் தாம் அவரின் முன் இகழ்க!
> என்னை, அவரொடு பட்டது? புன்னை
> விறல் பூங் கமழ் கானல் வீங்கு நீர்ச் சேர்ப்ப!
> உறற்பால யார்க்கும் உறும்.

118. Even though cows are of many colours
     Milk they give is not and charity similarly'
     Is of one quality but its methodology
     Differs as there are cows different.

Cows anywhere in the world are of different colours and sizes. But the milk they yield is only white in colour. So is charity which meant to help poor and the needy. But the agencies who extend charity differ from one another as cows differ.

> ஆ வேறு உருவின ஆயினும், ஆ பயந்த
> பால் வேறு உருவின அல்லவாம்; பால்போல்
> ஒருதன்மைத்து ஆகும் அறம்; நெறி, ஆபோல்,
> உருவு பலகொளால், ஈங்கு.

119. Who has been free from abuse in the word?
     And who hasn't adopted trickery in life?
     Who hasn't undergone sufferings in life?
     And Who has enjoyed wealth until their last days?

Series of questions in the stanza imply that all persons in average life either get abused or employed trickery or undergone sufferings or get deprived of wealth in their old age. This is the nature of life destined on almost everybody in the world.

யாஅர், உலகத்து ஓர் சொல் இல்லார்? தேருங்கால்
யாஅர், உபாயத்தின் வாழாதார்? யாஅர்,
இடையாக இன்னாதது எய்தாதார்? யாஅர்,
கடைபோகச் செல்வம் உய்த்தார்?

120. In analyzing, be aware that one's deeds alone
Go along with him but nothing else and the body
Which he safeguarded and beautified is of no use
When God of death snatches away his life.

When human life is snatched away by God of Death, what goes along with is that man's deeds alone be evil or good and nothing else. These deeds of him will proportionately yield good or bad in his next birth. Hence, desirable quality of a person is to do noble and benevolent deeds.

தாம் செய் வினை அல்லால், தம்மொடு செல்வது மற்று
யாங்கணும் தேரின், பிறிது இல்லை; ஆங்குத் தாம்
போற்றிப் புனைந்த உடம்பும் பயன் இன்றே,
கூற்றம் கொண்டு ஓடும் பொழுது.

☙ ♦ ❖ ♦ ❧

Chapter 13 - Fear of Evil deeds
***

Theme of the following ten stanzas is about the need for fearing to do evil deeds and harm to others. Let there be no harm not only to fellow beings but also to animals and birds. Love that is preached here is extended to animal and avian beings.

121. Graveyards contain corpses of persons
     Immersed in household misery not in renunciation;
     But the abdomen of unwise non-vegetarians
     Is a Cremation ground for carcass of beasts and
                                                              birds.

What the poem indicates is that the act of killing birds and beasts is highly abominable cruelty and to be avoided. Persons who have no knowledge of heavenly abode will relish in eating the flesh. Hence they are unwise and their evil action is highly detestable.

    துக்கத்துள் தூங்கி, துறவின்கண் சேர்கலா
    மக்கட் பிணத்த, சுடுகாடு;-தொக்க
    விலங்கிற்கும் புள்ளிற்கும் காடே, புலம் கெட்ட
    புல்லறிவாளர் வயிறு.

122. Those who cage birds such as *pheasants* and *kaadai*
     That live in bee – humming forests are bound
     To suffer with legs enchained, hard work
     As slaves in rocky terrains and wet fields.

Birds and animals are kept in cages as pets in houses. Even though they are looked after well, little we realize that such caged life is really an imprisonment for those poor and innocent creatures. The poem says that for such an offence, a man who does it, is bound to suffer in his next birth with his legs enchained.

He will also be made to work harsh in rocky ground and in wet fields. The implication is that we should not capture birds and animals that are leading a care free life in their natural habitat.

> இரும்பு ஆர்க்கும் காலர் ஆய், ஏதிலார்க்கு ஆள் ஆய்,
> கரும்பு ஆர் கழனியுள் சேர்வர்;-சுரும்பு ஆர்க்கும்
> காட்டுள் ஆய் வாழும் சிவலும் குறும்பூழும்
> கூட்டுள் ஆய்க் கொண்டு வைப்பார்.

123. If evil deeds of yore such as eating crabs
    By breaking their legs, reflect in this birth
    Such a man would be miserably leprotic with all
                                                fingers
    Maimed and rotten except the palm only.

Here in this stanza, crab is only a specimen. What applies to it is so, to all other creatures. One should not indulge in killing these innocent creatures. Violation of this ethical diktat may result in the offender in next birth getting a horrible disease known as leprosy. This warning is an evidence how far the poet wants us to avoid the habit of killing and eating aquatic reptiles such as crabs and fishes. Non-violence and vegetarianism are preached here.

> அக்கேபோல் அங்கை ஒழிய, விரல் அழுகி,
> துக்கத் தொழுநோய் எழுபவே-அக் கால்,
> அலவனைக் காதலித்துக் கால் முறித்துத் தின்ற
> பழவினை வந்து அடைந்தக்கால்.

124. Even soft ghee when gets melted
    Would burn the skin and hurt a man into pain;
    Similarly if honest persons join with bad elements
    They will also become evil-doers and hurt others.

In keeping company with evil men, even good persons will become bad. Hence what is implied here is that good and honest man should keep the bad elements at a distance; shouldn't have any truck with them. Ghee is a good edible; when it gets heated, it burns. Persons are generally good. But when joins with bad elements, they too become bad.

> நெருப்பு அழல் சேர்ந்தக்கால், நெய் போல்வதூஉம்
> எரிப்பச் சுட்டு, எவ்வ நோய் ஆக்கும்;-பரப்பக்
> கொடு வினையர் ஆகுவர், கோடாரும், கோடிக்
> கடு வினையர் ஆகியார்ச் சார்ந்து.

125. Intimacy with noble persons, like waxing moon
 Is bound to grow gradually by stages but
 Contact with low-bred will fade and sink
 Like waning moon on the sky.

Intimacy with noble and virtuous persons is encouraged. It is obvious therefore that persons of low caliber have to be kept at a distance. Friendship with ignoble persons is bound to gradually diminish of its importance as the waning moon on the sky.

> பெரியவர் கேண்மை, பிறை போல, நாளும்
> வரிசை வரிசையா நந்தும்; வரிசையால்,
> வான் ஊர் மதியம்போல் வைகலும் தேயுமே,
> தானே, சிறியார் தொடர்பு.

126. Listen, my dear! You have joined with a man
 Assuming him virtuous; but if virtue isn't found in him
 He is like a man who saw a snake within
 A copper vessel when he expected sandal paste in it.

One can hold any number of acquaintances but holding friendship must be with a few. Without checking the antecedents of a man, friendship with him may be unpleasant. Hence what is implied here is that one must not only be careful in cultivating friendship but must be afraid of camaraderie with evil persons.

> சான்றோர் என மதித்துச் சார்ந்தாய்மன்; சார்ந்தாய்க்குச்
> சான்றாண்மை சார்ந்தார்கண் இல் ஆயின்; சார்ந்தோய்! கேள்:
> சாந்து அகத்து உண்டு என்று, செப்புத் திறந்து, ஒருவன்
> பாம்பு கண்டன்னது உடைத்து.

127. Ye, Lord of a country where precious ruby
 Twinkle at the foot of hills ! Listen, who
 Is talented to study a man's mind and be aware
 Mind and actions of people are different from one another.

Mostly among many persons, mind and actions do not go together. They do not always correlate with one another. Hence efforts have to be made to ascertain whether a man is good and dignified before befriending him. Otherwise, it may even happen that his friendship may betray us at any time. In fact, there is no evil so great as holding a friendship without due enquiry.

யாஅர், ஒருவர் ஒருவர்தம் உள்ளத்தைத்
தேரும் துணைமை உடையவர்?-சாரல்
கன மணி நின்று இமைக்கும் நாட! கேள்:-மக்கள்
மனம் வேறு; செய்கையும் வேறு.

128. Ye, Lord of a hill where the water from falls
 Sideline the mud, a close link with those who
 Falsely befriending devoid of genuine intimacy
 Will give them a blot on their mind.

Hence one should avoid such false friendship. The friendship of those who do not hold true intimacy but prove to be unreliable and ingratitude will remain in your mind as an inerasable blot. What is counseled here is that one should hold no link with hypocrites. Last line in Tamil is an echo of Kural-34.

உள்ளத்தால் நள்ளாது, உறுதித் தொழிலர் ஆய்,
கள்ளத்தால் நட்டார் கழி கேண்மை-தெள்ளிப்
புனற் செதும்பு நின்று அலைக்கும் பூங் குன்ற நாட!
மனத்துக்கண் மாசு ஆய்விடும்.

129. If a man's sharp raised sword falls in the hands of a foe
 That will truly reduce the man's strength and likewise
 Benefits endowed on illiterates are meant
 To affect life, terrestrial and celestial, leave them off so.

If the sword of a fighter falls on the hands of an enemy, the fighter's strength will go off. Similarly if an idiotic person is helped, he would do actions detrimental to heaven and earth. Hence it is desirable that no help need be given to wily idiots. In other words, those who helped the vicious persons will suffer more than the persons who lost swords in the hands of their enemy.

> ஓக்கிய ஒள் வாள் தன் ஒன்னார் கைப் பட்டக்கால்,
> ஊக்கம் அழிப்பதூஉம் மெய் ஆகும்;-ஆக்கம்
> இருமையும் சென்று சுடுதலால், நல்ல
> கருமமே, கல்லார்கண் தீர்வு.

130. O! mind! You haven't given up passion from wife!
Neither from children and how long to live for them?
Even if little the benefit and charity done for others
Will be accounted better in your after-life.

The poem is purported to have been addressed by the poet to his mind. The substance is that any average man has a passion for his wife and children. According to the poet, this worldly attachment will never be of any use to a man's after – life. If he is charitable in worldly life, that charity will lead him to a happy and celestial life. Hence it is advised that he should be benevolent and charitable to others.

> மனைப் பாசம் கைவிடாய்! மக்கட்கு என்று ஏங்கி,
> எனைத்து ஊழி வாழ்தியோ?-நெஞ்சே!-எனைத்தும்
> சிறு வரையே ஆயினும், செய்த நன்று அல்லால்,
> உறு பயனோ இல்லை, உயிர்க்கு.

☙ ✦ ❖ ✦ ❧

Chapter 14 - Education
***

Keynote of this chapter is to educate ourselves with the books of Ethics and of material wealth. Even though education is meant to everybody, here it is referred to the king only, hoping that what is applicable to the ruler of a country is as well applicable to his citizens also. It should be deemed that the substance of this chapter is addressed commonly to everybody. Unless specifically counseled to the king and kingship, all the other matters that are referred to here, are meant to be understood by the entire public.

131. Beauty of hair, linings of dress, applying of turmeric
 Do not make up real beauty at all but conscientiously
 To say I am honest, good and impartial
 That education alone is actually a real beauty.

Dressing with chosen costumes and application of the best cosmetics do not make a person attractive and beautiful. Exceeding beauty is education itself that induces a knowledge that both men and women must be good in following justice and impartiality.

குஞ்சி அழகும், கொடுந் தானைக் கோட்டழகும்,
மஞ்சள் அழகும், அழகு அல்ல; நெஞ்சத்து,
'நல்லம் யாம்' என்னும் நடுவு நிலைமையால்,
கல்வி அழகே அழகு.

132. Bestows the blessings of the world and never
 Decreases when teach others, brings repute and never
 Goes off in life time and so in the world, never
 I see any except than education to erase ignorance.

Education would provide worldly benevolence; it would not decrease because of teaching it to others. It would provide a reputation to those who learnt it and highlight their eminence. Therefore the poet says that nowhere else in the whole world, he has seen any medicine that could cure the ailment of ignorance.

இம்மை பயக்குமால்; ஈயக் குறைவு இன்றால்;
தம்மை விளக்குமால்; தாம் உளராக் கேடு இன்றால்;
எம்மை உலகத்தும் யாம் காணேம், கல்விபோல்
மம்மர் அறுக்கும் மருந்து.

133. Learned men treat the salt born of brackish land
As more valuable than paddy harvested of fertile
                                                                soil;
Similar is honour to bestow on educated persons
Even if they are born of a low level group.

Salt is gathered from salt-pans of a brackish land. But being aware of its importance as an additive in all kinds of food and eatables, it is highly valued as an ingredient. Similarly even though a few educated persons are born of lower caste, they deserve a treatment, dignified and honourable in our society. It is a standard education that elevate them in society.

களர் நிலத்துப் பிறந்த உப்பினைச் சான்றோர்
விளை நிலத்து நெல்லின் விழுமிதாக் கொள்வர்;
கடை நிலத்தோர் ஆயினும், கற்று அறிந்தோரைத்
தலை நிலத்து வைக்கப்படும்.

134. If garnered, cant be robbed, if given to others it
Won't go off and even angry king can't confiscate
Wealth of education and so what one should
Leave behind to his children is academic properties.

Education cannot be robbed and if accredited with others it won't decrease. If a king is retributive against educated, he cannot deprive that man of his education. Hence the sole property to leave behind for one's own children, is nothing but an asset of a sound education.

> வப்புழிக் கோட்படா; வாய்த்து ஈயின், கேடு இல்லை;
> மிக்க சிறப்பின் அரசர் செறின், வவ்வார்;
> எச்சம் என ஒருவன் மக்கட்குச் செய்வன
> விச்சை; மற்று அல்ல, பிற.

135. Education is limitless but not so the days for learned
To think deeply, ailments are also plenty in life and so
Wise men learn those that are relevant and
 selective
As a swan that drinks only milk eliminating water.

Education is boundless. But a man's age is limited. To think correctly, even in the short duration of one's own life, diseases are many to interrupt. Hence great men would learn those that are useful, relevant and selective by omitting the trash and irrelevant as a swan that drinks milk only after eliminating water. Swan eliminating water from adulterated milk is not known whether it is true or not excepting literary references. May be apocryphal. But this allusion helps us to very well understand the substance of the poem.

> கல்வி கரை இல; கற்பவர் நாள் சில;
> மெல்ல நினைக்கின், பிணி பல; தெள்ளிதின்
> ஆராய்ந்து அமைவுடைய கற்பவே, நீர் ஒழியப்
> பால் உண் குருகின் தெரிந்து.

136. Nobody rebukes a boatman if he is found to be
A man of low caste and cross the river;
To get benevolent ideas from a low born but scholarly
Is also alike crossing the river with his help.

Even if a low caste man row the boat to cross the river, we would not reject but accept his services. In the same way, even if any learned man is from a depressed class, we should be ready to listen his benevolent counseling. He is dignified because of his education if not because of his birth.

> தோணி இயக்குவான், தொல்லை வருணத்து,
> காணின், கடைப்பட்டான் என்று இகழார்; காணாய்!
> அவன் துணையா ஆறு போயற்றே, நூல் கற்ற
> மகன் துணையா நல்ல கொளல்.

137. If only the demi-gods-living paradise is sweeter
Than the assemblage of those who are learned from
Ancient works, devoid of enmity and sharp-witted
Sit amongst happily to discuss, let us see it.

Learned wise-men, harmonious and sharp – witted sit amongst themselves and discuss happily with one another. If anybody says that the blessings of paradise are better than the delightful scholarly assemblage, the poet says that he will see and consider it. What the poem implies is that paradise is in no way better than the conclave of brilliant and outstanding scholars.

> தவல் அருந் தொல் கேள்வித் தன்மை உடையார்,
> இகல் இலர், எஃகு உடையார், தம்முள் குழீஇ,
> நகலின் இனிதுஆயின், காண்பாம், அகல் வானத்து
> உம்பர் உறைவார் பதி.

138. Ye, lord of the shores of roaring waves! Intimacy of
Learned is like tasting the sugarcane from
Top to bottom and the contact with low elements
Is like chewing the cane from bottom to top.

When tasting the sugarcane from top to bottom, it will be slightly bitter at the outset and will be sweeter by stages. So is the intimacy with the learned and wise. But a contact with unwise loafers will be sweet at the beginning but will become lesser and lesser to end with bitterness. It is desirable therefore that our association must be cultivated only with educated and good men.

கனை கடல் தண் சேர்ப்ப! கற்று அறிந்தார் கேண்மை
நுனியின் கரும்பு தின்றற்றே; நுனி நீக்கித்
தூரின் தின்றன்ன தகைத்துஅரோ, பண்பு இலா
ஈரம் இலாளர் தொடர்பு.

139. If matured and coloured flower of *Paathiri* is put
Into a pot of cold water, it would make the water fra
grant;
Similar will be the growth of wisdom and
knowledge
To even illiterates if only they move with learned
wise.

New water pots made of mud are capable of getting them absorbed with the sweet smell of *paathiri* flowers. Similarly even if illiterate persons keep company with scholarly men, they would also be benefitted with wisdom and knowledge.

கல்லாரே ஆயினும் கற்றாரைச் சேர்ந்து ஒழுகின்,
நல்லறிவு நாளும் தலைப்படுவர்-தொல் சிறப்பின்
ஒள் நிறப் பாதிரிப்பூச் சேர்தலால் புத்தோடு
தண்ணீர்க்குத் தான் பயந்தாங்கு.

140. Among books countless, devoid of learning
Spiritual treatise but browsing worldly wise works
Will make a hullabaloo but nobody seems to know
The way of weaning away from such susceptibilities.

Average men of work a - day world are susceptible to the books of material possessions and physical comfort. They simply make a genial hullabaloo and keep themselves satisfied with the contents of those ordinary texts. It is a pity that nobody seems to know the importance of learning spiritual treatises.

அலகு சால் கற்பின், அறிவன் நூல் கல்லாது,
உலக நூல் ஓதுவது எல்லாம், கலகல
கூஉம் துணைஅல்லால், கொண்டு, தடுமாற்றம்
போஒம் துணை அறிவார் இல்.

ஃ ❖ ❖ ஃ

Chapter 15 - Quality of those born in good family
***

Biologists observe that the gene of a person controls the development of good qualities that are passed on to the children from their parents. So the genes have something to do with the quality and temperament of younger generation. Their behaviour therefore is the hallmark of the family to which they belong. This is the theme of the following stanzas.

141. Even when misery of hunger over whelms, no lion
 Will ever consume the sprawling green grass;
 So also the members nobly – born won't give up
 Their dignity even when suffer of ill health and
 poverty.

Lion won't eat grass. It will leave it for animals lesser in size and strength such as goats, bulls and cows. In the same way men who are born of dignified families will never stoop to do any mean or evil actions against anybody. Even in extreme poverty and poor health, they wouldn't do any evil. That is their dignified propriety.

உடுக்கை உலறி உடம்பு அழிந்தக்கண்ணும்,
குடிப் பிறப்பாளர் தம் கொள்கையின் குன்றார்;
இடுக்கண் தலைவந்தக்கண்ணும், அரிமா
கொடிப் புல் கறிக்குமோ மற்று?

142. Ye, the Lord of steep hills that embrace the sky
 Three qualities, virtue, gentility, good conduct
 would be
 Found among those born in noble families
 And not in others even if they're fabulously
 wealthy.

Excellent qualities such as virtue, gentleness and good conduct would naturally be found among those who are born in standard families. Among others, even if they are exceedingly rich, these noble qualities would not be found. Qualities high or low depend upon status of the families according to the poet. Exceptionally there may be a good person from a bad family or vice versa. It has to be assumed that the author doesn't discount it. Moreover, exception cannot be the rule.

> சான்றாண்மை, சாயல், ஒழுக்கம், இவை மூன்றும்
> வான் தோய் குடிப் பிறந்தார்க்கு அல்லது,- வான் தோயும்
> மை தவழ் வெற்ப!-படாஅ, பெருஞ் செல்வம்
> எய்தியக்கண்ணும், பிறர்க்கு.

143. Those born of noble families follow the etiquette
Of standing from seat, receiving guests and
Bidding farewell but such discipline can't
Be identified with those of mean-minded persons.

Persons who are good and are bad are the same in form, shape and even in speech. But this is not to consider them on equal level. It is through their actions only, they must be separately understood. Those who do not follow the three practices at home on the arrival of guests are obviously bad elements. Men of dignified families, even if they are very rich, follow this custom and prove them to be worthy of being appreciated. Standing up, welcoming with folded hands and bidding farewell are the three practices.

> இருக்கை எழலும், எதிர் செலவும், ஏனை
> விடுப்ப ஒழிதலோடு, இன்ன, குடிப் பிறந்தார்
> குன்றா ஒழுக்கமாக் கொண்டார்; கயவரோடு
> ஒன்றா உணரற்பாற்று அன்று.

144. Doing good will be deemed natural and if bad,
It will be highlighted and be put to shame;
Hence what gain is it to be reaped
In being born in an all- knowing good family?

What the poem implies is that if low-bred people do all kinds of evil, the public wouldn't take it seriously, stating that such bad quality is their nature. Even if there is a minor lapse on the higher ups the society will highlight it and blame them. So what is the use of being born in a good family?. This doesn't mean that the author dislikes those who are born in a good family. Seemingly a dislike towards good family is a figure of speech.

The poem seems not to be depreciating the bad qualities. Nor appreciating good qualities. This method of conveying ideas in a seemingly negative manner is a figure of speech in which apparent censure adroitly suggest the opposite.

> நல்லவை செய்யின் இயல்பு ஆகும்; தீயவை
> பல்லவர் தூற்றும் பழி ஆகும்; எல்லாம்
> உண்ரும் குடிப் பிறப்பின் ஊதியம் என்னோ
> புணரும் ஒருவர்க்கு எனின்?

145. Fear of being uneducated and of being criminal
 Fear of bad words and fear of being incapable of
 Whether I help the poor or not make the good people
 Worried like those who travel in mid-sea in a boat.

Men of bad quality would never be worried about following any of the noble practices. Whether we would be able to follow or not is a kind of benevolent fear which really good people have in mind and that is why the poet compares them to a set of persons who fear middle of the ocean in a small boat. The figure of speech applied in the previous stanza is followed here.

> கல்லாமை அச்சம்; கயவர் தொழில் அச்சம்;
> சொல்லாமையுள்ளும் ஓர் சோர்வு அச்சம்; எல்லாம்
> இரப்பார்க்கு ஒன்று ஈயாமை அச்சம்; மரத்தார் இம்
> மாணாக் குடிப் பிறந்தார்.

146. Ye, the Lord of a coast where roars the sea
With rubies and pearls! Benefits to kith and kin
Words pleasing, alms offering, pure in mind and heart
Are the qualities noble, found among families dignified.

Implication is that qualities cherishable noted in the poem are not found among the low- bred people. However these are all virtues to be followed by everybody else is obvious. Not that the poet decries the low-bred persons. But he speaks highly of the noble families.

இன நன்மை, இன்சொல், ஒன்று ஈதல், மற்று ஏனை
மன நன்மை, என்று இவை எல்லாம்,- கன மணி
முத்தோடு இமைக்கும் முழங்கு உவரித் தண் சேர்ப்ப!
இற் பிறந்தார்கண்ணே உள.

147. Even though structure is decayed, over come
By white ants, a house may have a safe corner.
To prevent raindrops and so will be the deeds of worthy
Families to do whatever have to do, despite their penury.

Persons born of noble families would do good and benevolent deeds, even though they suffer due to poverty. Poems 148,150,153,184 and 185 explain the same idea in different versions. To a discriminating reader, this may be appear to be repetitive but what should be kept in mind is, that each poem is said to have been composed by individual poets and hence the similarity of one and the same idea.

செய்கை அழிந்து, சிதல் மண்டிற்றுஆயினும்,
பெய்யா ஒரு சிறை பேர் இல் உடைத்து ஆகும்;
எவ்வம் உழந்தக்கடைத்தும், குடிப் பிறந்தார்
செய்வர், செயற்பாலவை.

148. Even if mythical snakes eclipse in a part
　　　Moon illumines the world with the other; similarly
　　　Those of noble families, despite their poverty
　　　Wouldn't hesitate to help the poor to the extent
　　　　　　　　　　　　　　　　　　　　possible.

Snakes referred to in the stanza are known as *Raagu* and *Kethu* in Indian almanacs. It is these stars that are responsible for a partial lunar eclipse. However with the other un eclipsed part, the moon illuminates the universe. Similarly persons born of noble and rich families would not stop extending some help or other to the needy in spite of their own limitations.

ஒரு புடை பாம்பு கொளினும், ஒரு புடை
அம் கண் மா ஞாலம் விளக்குறூஉம் திங்கள்போல்,-
செல்லாமை செல்வன் நேர் நிற்பினும், ஒப்புரவிற்கு
ஒல்கார்-குடிப் பிறந்தார்.

149. What high - bred do even in indigence
　　　Lowbred wouldn't do even in prosperity,
　　　As a deer, though sportive doesn't charge fiercely
　　　As much as a horse that does swiftly in action.

This poem is meant to highlight the dignified rich who would extend benefits to the poor even when they are not resourceful. They are discriminated from the low-bred persons who would not offer anything to anybody even when they are rich and resourceful.

செல்லா இடத்தும் குடிப் பிறந்தார் செய்வன,
செல் இடத்தும் செய்யார், சிறியவர்;-புல்வாய்
பருமம் பொறுப்பினும், பாய் பரிமாபோல்
பொரு முரண் ஆற்றுதல் இன்று.

150. Men of noble families, even when they're poor
　　　To those who come as a last resort, provide some
　　　　　　　　　　　　　　　　　　　　thing
　　　As a wide river-bed yield a good water, if dug
　　　Despite conditions of drought prevail.

Once again the charitable quality of the good - minded persons of noble families is illustrated.

எற்று ஒன்றும் இல்லா இடத்தும், குடிப் பிறந்தார்
அற்றுத் தற் சேர்ந்தார்க்கு அசைவிடத்து ஊற்று ஆவர்;
அற்றக் கடைத்தும் அகல் யாறு அகழ்ந்தக்கால்,
தெற்றெனத் தெள் நீர் படும்.

Chapter - 16 Great Persons
***

Greatness comes more because of nobility and benevolence than of geneology and birth. Following stanzas illustrate this general truth.

151. The Moon that showers its bright rays from the sky
And great men in the world are equal in a level;
While the moon in its sphere bear its blot,
The great wouldn't bear any stigma, if it occurs.

The Moon illumines the universe by its bright rays, eliminating darkness. Similarly, great men would wipe off the darkness of ignorance from the minds of other men. Herein lies the base for comparison between the moon and great men. But still great men are better than the moon. A blot is congenital in the lunar surface. Great men have no such stigma and even if it occurs in the course of their life, they would not brook it. It is in this respect, they appear better than the moon.

> அம் கண் விசும்பின் அகல் நிலாப் பாரிக்கும்
> திங்களும் சான்றோரும் ஒப்பர்மன்; திங்கள்
> மறு ஆற்றும்; சான்றோர் அஃது ஆற்றார்; தெருமந்து
> தேய்வர், ஒரு மாசு உறின்.

152. Arrows' failure in piercing the lion is
Better than its success in getting a fox gored.
So unmindful of success or failure
Great men would aim at big things devoid of injustice.

Great men would relish to do big things that are blameless and justifiable. Achievement is not a criterion but an attempt itself is big, provided it is free from any blame or offensiveness.

Comparable to the Kural-772. Better it is to hold an arrow that has missed an Elephant than that which has killed a deer.

> இசையும் எனினும், இசையாதுஎனினும்,
> வசை தீர எண்ணுவர், சான்றோர்;-விசையின்
> நரிமா உளம் கிழித்த அம்பினின் தீதோ,
> அரிமாப் பிழைப்ப எய்த கோல்?

153. Even if acutely poor appear as a skeleton
 Great men would never violate good deeds;
 Holding the fleeting mind with a rope of con
 science,
 Whatever to be done, they would do within their
 limits.

Great men may suffer due to acute poverty; may even appear as skeleton. But still they would not do anything against good deeds. Sometimes mind may vacillate in doing between good and bad. But they will control it with conscience and do whatever good they could within their possibility. Even if they suffer for want of resources, great men would not do anything wrong or unjustifiable.

> நரம்பு எழுந்து நல்கூர்ந்தார் ஆயினும், சான்றோர்
> குரம்பு எழுந்து குற்றம் கொண்டு ஏறார்; உரம் கவரா,
> உள்ளம் எனும் நாரினால் கட்டி, உளவரையால்
> செய்வர், செயற்பாலவை.

154. Acquaint even for a day with great men would
 Enable you to grapple with their friendship
 Ye, the Lord of the hill! Trodden path will
 Appear even on a stony rock.

Not necessarily one should go to nurture an acquaintance with a man for a long duration. Lengthy duration of closeness of a man doesn't ensure a longevity of friendship. Constant walking of persons on a rock may create a footpath. It doesn't give the shape of a highway. So enough it is even for a day to hold intimacy if only that man is great and eminent.

> செல்வுழிக்கண் ஒருநாள் காணினும், சான்றவர்
> தொல் வழிக் கேண்மையின் தோன்றப் புரிந்து யாப்பர்;
> நல் வரை நாட!-சில நாள் அடிப்படின்,
> கல் வரையும் உண்டாம், நெறி.

155. Even when an illiterate meaninglessly
    Speaks to an inane crowd, great men
    Avoiding to put him publicly into ridicule
    Regretfully listen to him with mercy.

An illiterate's aimless and informal speech to a mob may very easily be put derisively into laughter. But great men won't do because of mercy to that illiterate, even though they found themselves hearing to his harangue regretfully vide Kural 401-Speaking without fullness of knowledge is like playing at chess without squares.

> புல்லா எழுத்தின் பொருள் இல் வறுங் கோட்டி,
> கல்லா ஒருவன் உரைப்பவும், கண் ஓடி,
> நல்லார் வருந்தியும் கேட்பரே, மற்று அவன்
> பல்லாருள் நாணல் பரிந்து.

156. Whether sugarcane is bitten or mashed in mill
    Or crushed in machine, its juice will be sweet.
    Great men too, even when others abuse and offend
    Would not impatiently retort and scold them.

Great men would not speak anything badly. They would withstand even anything offensive and on no account retort anybody abusingly. Tit for tat is not their policy. They would never be mouthing harsh words against those who vilify them.

கடித்துக் கரும்பினைக் கண் தகர நூறி,
இடித்து, நீர் கொள்ளினும் இன் சுவைத்தே ஆகும்;
வடுப்பட வைது இறந்தக்கண்ணும், குடிப் பிறந்தார்
கூறார், தம் வாயின் சிதைந்து.

157. Great men infallible, prevent detestable
 Neither rob nor drink toddy and never
 Speak ill of and insult others and never
 They Utter lie and no regrets even in poverty.

Virtues and habits normally followed by great men are listed out in this stanza. Those who renounce family life and seek isolation for sainthood are also expected to observe these practices. Shall we say then all great men are saints or all saints are great men? It behoves us to think of it. There are those who are apparently saints but lead a life of family men. Opposite to this is the saintly life of adorable householders. It is about these great men, the poem speaks of.

கள்ளார்; கள் உண்ணார்; கடிவ கடிந்து ஒரீஇ,
எள்ளிப் பிறரை இகழ்ந்து உரையார்; தள்ளியும்,
வாயின் பொய் கூறார்;-வடு அறு காட்சியார்-
சாயின், பரிவது இலர்.

158. If a person behaves deferentially as
 A deaf in hearing others' secrets and as
 A blind in ogling at other's wife and as
 A dumb in back-biting, no need to counsel him.

All these desirable qualities belong to great men. If only any individual follows these appreciable traits, he is certainly a great man and worthy of being emulated by others.

பிறர் மறையின்கண் செவிடு ஆய், திறன் அறிந்து
ஏதிலார் இற்கண் குருடன் ஆய், தீய
புறங்கூற்றின் மூங்கை ஆய், நிற்பானேல், யாதும்
அறம் கூற வேண்டா, அவற்கு.

159. If one calls on unethical men frequently
 They deem him as a man of want and pre-emptively
 Ridicule but even if he needs help, great men
 Would do, not once but at every time he goes to them.

Lower quality of unethical men and esteemable virtues of great ethical men are juxtaposed here. Men of lower calibre would be negligent of those who come frequently to them for getting some favours. But men of nobility would generously oblige those who come often with a request for help.

> பல் நாளும் சென்றக்கால், பண்பு இலார் தம்முழை,
> 'என்னானும் வேண்டுப' என்று இகழ்ப; 'என்னானும்
> வேண்டினும் நன்று மற்று' என்று, விழுமியோர்
> காண்தொறும் செய்வர், சிறப்பு.

160. There are those who steadfastly holding a rich man
 Who is immodest and keep his tail to lead their life;
 If they attach themselves with men of high caliber
 It's almost like a rich mine to reap from.

Theme of this stanza is that benefits accrue to a man from immodest persons will be lesser than what they are likely to get from persons of high caliber. The term *'nalla kulam'* of the Tamil text is purposely rendered here as 'high calibre' and not translated literally.

> 'உடையார் இவர்' என்று, ஒருதலையாப் பற்றி,
> கடையாயார் பின் சென்று வாழ்வர்; உடைய
> பிலம் தலைப்பட்டது போலாதே, நல்ல
> குலம் தலைப்பட்ட இடத்து.

Chapter 17 - Offending not the Great
***

How to behave with great people without insulting them is the theme of this chapter. The term 'great' includes elders, high officials, authorities, seniors and leaders.

161. Ye! Lord of hilly country of roaring cascade!
     One should avoid disgusting behavior with elders
     Hoping they would tolerate; if they don't,
     Its consequences can t easily be brushed aside.

One should be cautious in offending great people. Taking for granted that they would bear with, if anything is done insultingly, consequences may be unbearable. Hence it is desirable that one should behave within the limits.

'பொறுப்பர்' என்று எண்ணி, புரை தீர்ந்தார் மாட்டும்
வெறுப்பன செய்யாமை வேண்டும்; வெறுத்தபின்,
ஆர்க்கும் அருவி அணி மலை நல் நாட!
பேர்க்குதல் யார்க்கும் அரிது.

162. Even though few impractical wise men
     Keep in friendship great men, whose
     Intimacy can't be gotten by gold
     Waste their time devoid of using them.

Friendship with great men, is very rare to obtain even at a considerable cost. Even after securing such a friendship, if anybody does not learn the ways of life, it is a sheer waste of time. One must keep in mind that there is no retirement for learning. Hence by listening to the elders, one should serve the purpose and spend his life purposefully.

பொன்னே கொடுத்தும், புணர்தற்கு அரியாரைக்
கொன்னே தலைக்கூடப் பெற்றிருந்தும், அன்னோ!
பயன் இல் பொழுதாக் கழிப்பரே-நல்ல
நயம் இல் அறிவினவர்.

163. Insult and excessive respect are shown
By men of average calibre; those who are great
And scholarly wouldn't take it to heart either
The eulogy or offence of such indisciplined persons.

Men of outstanding calibre would not mind whether they are eulogized or offended. They are above these things and mindful of their own lofty ideals and achievements. Ordinary people are normally susceptible either to insults or respects.

அவமதிப்பும், ஆன்ற மதிப்பும், இரண்டும்,
மிகை மக்களால் மதிக்கற்பால; நயம் உணரா,
கை அறியா, மாக்கள் இழிப்பும் எடுத்து ஏத்தும்,
வையார், வடித்த நூலார்.

164. Even if sparkling cobra lie deep in rocky fissure
Afraid it's to hear thunder - sound even from afar;
If great men are furious, those men who acutely
                                                offended
Cannot escape even if well-protected they are.

Implication is that great men should not seriously be offended. Their anger may bring in to the offenders a lot of undesirable consequences. This thunder that sounds from afar and the anger that great men hold are alike.

விரி நிற நாகம் விடர் உளதேனும்,
உருமின் கடுஞ் சினம் சேண் நின்றும், உட்கும்;
அருமை உடைய அரண் சேர்ந்தும் உய்யார்,
பெருமை உடையார் செறின்.

165. Few men claiming 'not known me', 'peerless I am'
 Such self-conceited claim is not real fame;
 To be recognized as rare and reputed person
 By versatile great men alone is real eminence.

Self adulation is undesirable. Anybody's worth has to be assessed and admired by men of versatility. That alone is real eminence. Egotism is undesirable and humbleness is appreciable.

'எம்மை அறிந்திலிர்; எம் போல்வார் இல்' என்று
தம்மைத் தாம் கொள்வது கோள் அன்று; தம்மை
அரியரா நோக்கி, அறன் அறியும் சான்றோர்,
பெரியராக் கொள்வது கோள்.

166. Ye, the Lord of a coastal region! Familiarity of the
 Lower people get decreased like a morning
 shadow;
 Intimacy of great veterans never minimize
 But as evening shadow goes on getting increased.

Therefore what the poem implies is that one should be very particular in befriending great people, as and when occasion arises. That is bound to be benevolent in all aspects.

நளிகடல் தண்சேர்ப்ப! நாள் நிழல் போல
விளியும் சிறியவர் கேண்மை-விளிவின்றி
அல்கு நிழல் போல் அகன்று அகன்று ஓடுமே
தொல் புகழாளர் தொடர்பு.

167. Fertile trees of cool green leaves that grow
 Around inside is a shelter for all who goes there;
 Similar benefit for all who move closer to the king
 And for husbands to enjoy the beauty of the
 comely ladies.

The courtiers who behave with the king do get things done. Husbands are privileged to move closer and enjoy their wives of attractive beauty. Similar happiness is for the public who go under the greenwood tree to enjoy cool shadow. Good conduct and modest behavior with great men such as Lords and Kings will bear fruit.

> மன்னர் திருவும், மகளிர் எழில் நலமும்,
> துன்னியார் துய்ப்பர்; தகல் வேண்டா;-துன்னிக்
> குழை கொண்டு தாழ்ந்த குளிர் மரம் எல்லாம்
> உழை, தம்கண் சென்றார்க்கு ஒருங்கு.

168. Ye, Lord of salt-borne coastal region ! Farewell
 Even from acute ignorants of knowable matters
 Will be painful and hence, better in a way
 Not to move closely and friendly with anybody.

Parting of the ways from unworthy and innocent people at times will be painful, because of habitual and casual affection. If that is so, it is implied that if one moves very closely with great men and then parting from them will be much more painful. That is why the poet says, as a solution it is better not to move with anybody. In other words, the poem also seems to imply that it is not desirable to keep friendship with whomsoever we meet. Be acquainted with all but friendliness must be with a chosen few. This poem is comparable to stanza – 247.

> தெரியத் தெரியும் தெரிவு இலார்க்கண்ணும்
> பெரிய, பெரும் படர் நோய் செய்யும்;-பெரிய
> உலவா இருங் கழிச் சேர்ப்ப!-யார் மாட்டும்
> கலவாமை கோடி உறும்.

169. Doesn't happen among great men, no regret
 Of days spent unlearnt, no days passed
 Without contacting great men, and
 No days gone off sans offering aid.

In analyzing qualities that are to be emulated from great men include not a day passed without reading, without moving some great men or other not without giving some possible aid to the poor. It goes without saying therefore that really great men regularly read, move with good people and help others.

> கல்லாது போகிய நாளும், பெரியவர்கண்
> செல்லாது வைகிய வைகலும், ஒல்வ
> கொடாஅது ஒழிந்த பகலும்,-உரைப்பின்,
> படாஅ ஆம், பண்புடையார் கண்.

170. Eminence of great men is their simplicity and the
    Duty of those avowing salvation is control of
    Senses and if rich men remove the sufferings
    Of their near and dear, they are all truly wealthy.

This stanza in a way enumerates the responsibilities of great men, saints and rich men. Simplicity along with the controlling of senses and helping tendency are the traits respectively of all these three categories of men.

> பெரியார் பெருமை சிறு தகைமை; ஒன்றிற்கு
> உரியார் உரிமை அடக்கம்; தெரியுங்கால்,
> செல்வம் உடையாரும் செல்வரே, தற்சேர்ந்தார்
> அல்லல் களைப எனின்.

Chapter 18 - Affinity with noble group
***

Maintaining affinity with men of nobility is the most desirable quality to be followed. This implies that one should keep undesirable persons at a distance.

171. Adoption of unruliness in immature age
    In the company of uncontrollable young men
    get annihilated if only they join with great men,
    As dew drops of grass vanish from the sunlight.

Young men, at an immature age sometimes fall into a group of unruly fellows. But subsequently if they get attached with great men, their evil behavior, if any would disappear as dew drops before sunlight.

> அறியாப் பருவத்து அடங்காரோடு ஒன்றி,
> நெறியல்ல செய்து ஒழுகியவ்வும், நெறி அறிந்த
> நற் சார்வு சார, கெடுமே-வெயில் முறுகப்
> புற் பனிப் பற்று விட்டாங்கு.

172. Be aware of charitable ways; fear
    The God of Death, bear others' hard words
    Protect yourself from deceit, abhor the friendship
    Of evil men and listen the counsel of Great men.

The stanza contains a list of doables to be done by both men and women.

> அறிமின், அற நெறி; அஞ்சுமின், கூற்றம்;
> பொறுமின், பிறர் கடுஞ் சொல்; போற்றுமின், வஞ்சம்;
> வெறுமின், வினை தீயார் கேண்மை; எஞ் ஞான்றும்
> பெறுமின், பெரியார் வாய்ச் சொல்.

173. Men suffer parting away from kinsfolk, diseases
 Acute and evils in life since the day of birth and so
 Let my mind be closer with great men who
 Knows that human birth is condemnable.

The poet says to himself that he must mentally be closely associated with great men because it is they who know and make me realise that human birth is condemnable. Parting away from kith and kin, physical sickness and other evils in the world are like impediments in one's own life. That is why the poet aspires a notional attachment with great men.

> அடைந்தார்ப் பிரிவும், அரும் பிணியும், கேடும்,
> உடங்கு, உடம்பு கொண்டார்க்கு உறலால், தொடங்கி,
> 'பிறப்பு இன்னாது' என்று உணரும் பேர் அறிவினாரை
> உறப் புணர்க, அம்மா, என் நெஞ்சு!

174. When deeply thinking, birth is repulsive
 But if one hold intimacy with good-hearted
 And virtuous men for ever in life
 Nobody would certainly hate it.

Typical ascetics hold an opinion than human life is problematic and hateful. That is why they pray God that they should not undergo a re-birth. But what the poet says here is even that human life can be made not only acceptable but even enjoyable if only the aspirants keep themselves in touch with great men. Their guidance would certainly counsel the aspirants to go on the right path.

> இறப்ப நினையுங்கால், இன்னாது எனினும்,
> பிறப்பினை யாரும் முனியார்-பிறப்பினுள்
> பண்பு ஆற்றும் நெஞ்சத்தவர்களோடு எஞ்ஞான்றும்
> நண்பு ஆற்றி நட்கப் பெறின்.

175. If drained water of a village joins with
　　　Clean water of a tank, it gets its name changed
　　　Even as holy and so if low level men join with
　　　Virtuous great, they would be ranked high as mount.

　　If waste water from the drain joins with the protected water of a tank, its name sewage gets changed. It may even be deemed a holy water- 'theertham' - if the tank is in the close vicinity of a temple. Similarly, those born of low-level would be considered as high as a mountain if only they get themselves closely associated with virtuous great men.

> ஊர் அங்கண நீர் உரவு நீர்ச் சேர்ந்தக்கால்,
> பேரும் பிறிது ஆகி, தீர்த்தம் ஆம்;-ஓரும்
> குல மாட்சி இல்லாரும் குன்றுபோல் நிற்பர்,
> நல மாட்சி நல்லாரைச் சார்ந்து.

176. Even a black stain in moon is also prayed
　　　Due to its location in illuminating lunar space;
　　　So also men of less virtue will be renowned
　　　If they hold intimacy with virtuous men.

　　Black stain is condemnable. But it is prayed because it is found within the moon. In the same way, men of even lesser dignity will get a name and fame if they are associated with outstanding men of great virtues. The dark spot or a stain on the moon appears to be in the shape of a hare and so in the Tamil original, it is referred to as such.

> ஒண் கதிர் வாள் மதியம் சேர்தலால், ஓங்கிய
> அம் கண் விசும்பின் முயலும் தொழப்படுடேம்;-
> குன்றிய சீர்மையர் ஆயினும், சீர் பெறுவர்,
> குன்று அன்னார் கேண்மை கொளின்.

177. Bit of water blended with milk will be
　　　Milk only and doesn't appear as water;
　　　So also the low calibre of small men won't
　　　Appear as such if associated with virtuous men.

What this stanza implies is if men of low level get associated with great men, the virtues of the great will pre-occupy the low-bred. Any evil found in lower man will not be highlighted by this modest association.

> பாலோடு அளாய நீர் பால் ஆகும் அல்லது,
> நீராய் நிறம் தெரிந்து தோன்றாதாம்;-தேரின்,
> சிறியார் சிறுமையும் தோன்றாதாம், நல்ல
> பெரியார் பெருமையைச் சார்ந்து.

178. In farm yard and in large fields, grass
Closer to stem part of trees wouldn't yield
To plough and so is the fury of foes that can't
Inflict upon weaklings closer to strong great men.

In fields and in dry lands, if the grass is closer to the trunk or stem of big trees, ploughs cannot go very near the tree and mow the grass. Similarly, if weak persons are closely moving with great virtuous men, no enemy can do anything against them.

> கொல்லை இரும் புனத்துக் குற்றி அடைந்த புல்
> ஒல்காவே ஆகும், உழவர் உழுபடைக்கு;
> மெல்லியரேஆயினும், நற் சார்வு சார்ந்தார்மேல்,
> செல்லாவாம், செற்றார் சினம்.

179. As paddy grows due to fertility of soil, men
Would become great due to their group benevolent;
As cyclic wind dislocate sea-faring ship
Men get spoiled if associated with vicious persons.

Excellence of becoming great with a group of virtuous men and badness in joining with vicious gang are explained in the stanza.

> நில நலத்தால் நந்திய நெல்லேபோல், தம்தம்
> குல நலத்தால் ஆகுவர், சான்றோர்; கல நலத்தைத்
> தீ வளி சென்று சிதைத்தாங்கு, சான்றாண்மை
> தீஇனம் சேரக் கெடும்.

180. When wild trees are burnt, along with, a few
Fragrant sandal and *Venkai* too get burned even
Even if men are inherently virtuous they
Reproached because of their bad company.

Agriculturists burn the wild bush and grass to reclaim a land for arable purposes. A few valuable sandal and *Venkai* trees (Pterocarpus bilobus) also may get burnt on that occasion. Similarly, by nature, a few persons may be good and virtuous. But if they keep a bad company, they will also be criticized if not condemned. Needless to say that it is desirable to keep bad elements at a distance.

மனத்தால் மறு இலரேனும், தாம் சேர்ந்த
இனத்தால் இகழப்படுவர்;-புனத்து
வெறி கமழ் சந்தனமும் வேங்கையும் வேமே
எறி புனம் தீப்பட்டக்கால்.

Chapter 19 - Lofty Grandeur
***

It is a matter of pride that comes due to a determination to do whatever that is possible in life. It is a grandeur for an individual to think and do liberally and to move freely with others. This chapter deals with the ways and means of attaining that grandeur.

181. Can't donate, and youth leaves me off
 Dear wife too unconcerned and so desirable it's
 After giving up a passion for leading this life
 And to go on securing a life of renunciation.

This stanza is purported to have been said by an individual to himself – almost like a soliloquy. Belief in after – life was predominant in those days and even deemed to be paradisical and hence this desire of an individual to seek the life of an ascetic.

> 'ஈதல் இசையாது; இளமை சேண் நீங்குதலால்,
> காதலவரும் கருத்து அல்லர்; காதலித்து,
> "ஆதும் நாம்" என்னும் அவாவினைக் கைவிட்டுப்
> போவதே போலும் பொருள்!'

182. Comfort and domestic life make the unwise
 Gleeful and to forget the dire consequences;
 Whosoever realize that those are inconstant
 And perishable are savants who never regrets.

Inclination towards an after - life is highlighted. According to this poem, domestic bliss is in no way better than ascetic life.

> 'இச் சார்வின் ஏமாந்தேம்; ஈங்கு அமைந்தேம்' என்று எண்ணிப்
> பொச்சாந்து ஒழுகுவர், பேதையார்; 'அச் சார்வு
> நின்றன போன்று நிலையா' என உணர்ந்தார்,
> என்றும் பரிவது இலர்.

183. Even as such as the life get changed
    Miseries too arise, in any, uninvited and hence
    Do lead your life wisely, devoid of any delusion
    Avoiding from any amount of lowliness.

Stature in life and prosperity in day to day affairs make a man cheerful and happy. But they are not permanent. Life and prosperity get dislocated slowly but surely. Hence the poet counsels us to lead a life wiser for reaching the other world without getting deluded into material prosperity.

மறுமைக்கு வித்து மயல் இன்றிச் செய்து,
சிறுமைப் படாதே, நீர் வாழ்மின், அறிஞராய்;-
நின்றுழி நின்றே நிறம் வேறு ஆம்; காரணம்
இன்றிப் பலவும் உள.

184. It's said, wells, even in drought generate water
    To be drawn and drunk by rural populace;
    Great men offer even in hard days, liberal donation
    Which, becomes rare in others even in their richness.

Those who are low in quality would not offer anything to others but great men would do even in their hard days; this is comparable to a public well which supplies water from its inner springs even in drought conditions. Such munificence is the grandeur of those great men.

'உறைப்பு அருங் காலத்தும், ஊற்று நீர்க் கேணி
இறைத்து உணினும், ஊர் ஆற்றும்' என்பர்; கொடைக்
                                                கடனும்,
சாஅயக்கண்ணும், பெரியார்போல் மற்றையார்
ஆஅயக்கண்ணும், அரிது.

185. Rivers in full, supply the water and quench our thirst
    But in dryness too, to a few thro their spring;
    Likewise, apart from liberal gift when in richness
    Great men do, as much as they could even in penury.

The grandeur of great men is explained here. Even when they suffer from depletion of wealth, they give as much as they could to a few, at least if not to many. This is like a river that supplies water thro its spring from the river - bed even during dry and water less days.

> உறு புனல் தந்து, உலகு ஊட்டி, அறும் இடத்தும்
> கல்லூற்றுழி ஊறும் ஆறேபோல், செல்வம்
> பலர்க்கு ஆற்றி, கெட்டு உலந்தக்கண்ணும், சிலர்க்கு ஆற்றிச்
> செய்வர், செயற்பாலவை.

186. Ye, Lord of high hills! Fault of eminent men will be
 Glaring as black scar of a burn on a white bull;
 If low fellows do, even a great blunder of killing
 That bull, such a fault of theirs will never appear at all

Even small offence of great men will be glaringly known, but even bigger offences of lower men will never appear at all. When an ox or bull get into a sickness, rural peasants will apply a red hot iron-rod on its body to get that animal cured.

> பெரு வரை நாட! பெரியார்கண் தீமை
> கரு நரைமேல் சூடேபோல் தோன்றும்; கரு நரையைக்
> கொன்றன்ன இன்னா செயினும், சிறியார்மேல்
> ஒன்றானும் தோன்றாக் கெடும்.

187. Even a level of friendship with unworthy loafers
 Is a matter of misery but even enmity with
 Great men who never do any offence either jokingly
 Or even sportively is a matter of pride and dignity.

Friendship with loafers is worse and so long as it continues, misery also will increase. The enmity we create with men of great eminence and fame will never do any harm but may even increase one's own pride. That is the grandeur of great men.

இசைந்த சிறுமை இயல்பு இலாதார்கண்
பசைந்த துணையும், பரிவு ஆம்; அசைந்த
நகையேயும் வேண்டாத நல் அறிவினார்கண்
பகையேயும் பாடு பெறும்.

188. Softness to gentle women but apart,
Fierce enmity to foes such as to instil fear
Into God of Death and deceitful to tricksters
And to the noble, be an exceedingly good man.

In a deeper scrutiny, the idea of fierce enmity to foes goes counter to the content of the famous Biblical statement, *whosoever smiteth thee on the right cheek, turn to him to the other one also* - Gospel of Matthew. Do these qualities are correct with the grandeur of great men?. However, the content of the poem is a practical counselling to an average world.

மெல்லிய நல்லாருள் மென்மை, அது இறந்து
ஒன்னாருள் கூற்று உட்கும் உட்கு உடைமை, எல்லாம்
சலவருள் சாலச் சலமே, நலவருள்
நன்மை, வரம்பாய் விடல்!

189. Even if one speaks furiously against
A known person and makes the listener confounded
He who doesn't feel inimical and get not perturbed
Is like a bright flame of the burning lamp.

This poem emphasizes the importance of holding one's own opinion in spite of what others say with vested interest. In a way, comparable to what Shakespeare says, *Take each man's censure but reserve thy judgment.* - Hamlet

கடுக்கி, ஒருவன் கடுங் குறளை பேசி,
மயக்கிவிடினும், மனப் பிரிப்பு ஒன்று இன்றி,
துளக்கம் இலாதவர், தூய மனத்தார்,
விளக்கினுள் ஒண் சுடரே போன்று.

190. Noble men consume their food only
 After having fed others freely and such
 A liberality will keep them free of three
 Follies until they breathe their last.

Three follies to which men are susceptible are lust, anger and spiritual delusion. Desirable quality for men and women is to share their food with others. Keeping the three follies at a distance is an additional credit to human beings.

முன் துற்றும் துற்றினை நாளும் அறம் செய்து,
பின் துற்றுத் துற்றுவர், சான்றவர்; அத் துற்று
முக் குற்றம் நீக்கி, முடியும் அளவு எல்லாம்
துக்கத்துள் நீக்கிவிடும்.

Chapter 20 - Efficiency of efforts
***

Instead of being submissive and inactive, one should make efforts to succeed in life. Effectiveness of efforts is the content of this chapter.

191. As sheet of grass get dried in a drying pond
    Effortless relatives eat what is given and suffer along;
    Will this folly of effortlessness be found among
    Those who work as busy as the keen eyed swordmen?

No. Those who are as busy and industrious as the alert and nimble eyes of a swordsmen will never be at the mercy of others. They will earn and take care of themselves. But those who are dull and effortless will always be dependent on other relatives and suffer in life. Skilfully brandishing and waving the sharp swords in hand was a kind of rural game in ancient Tamil land. This swordsmanship and fencing are alike.

கோள் ஆற்றக் கொள்ளாக் குளத்தின்கீழ்ப் பைங் கூழ்போல்,
கேள் ஈவது உண்டு, கிளைகளோ துஞ்சுப;
வாள் ஆடு கூத்தியர் கண்போல் தடுமாறும்
தாளாளர்க்கு உண்டோ, தவறு?

192. A Plant with its swaying branch on the way
    When grown strong would be a thick stump to
    Shackle even an elephant and if one keeps
    Himself well and high, his life too would be as such.

What this stanza attempts to say is that a sincere effort of an individual, if self-sustained will prove to be highly progressive, despite some setbacks at the outset. One should not depend on others but take efforts to attain progress.

ஆடு கோடு ஆகி அதரிடை நின்றதூஉம்,
காழ் கொண்டகண்ணே, களிறு அணைக்கும் கந்து ஆகும்;-
வாழ்தலும் அன்ன தகைத்தே, ஒருவன்தான்
தாழ்வு இன்றித் தன்னைச் செயின்.

193. Even strong tiger, if deprived of carcass
Will survive by eating even a little frog; hence
Consider not any vocation as lesser and paltry
Even that, by effort sincere, would grow well.

Even a humble enterprise would prove to be really successful, if only it is supplemented by sincere effort. To cite an example, the Infosys of Bangalore was started with an outlay of forty thousand rupees invested by four partners but its present worth is multicrores.

உறு புலி ஊன் இரை இன்றி, ஒருநாள்
சிறு தேரை பற்றியும் தின்னும்;-அறிவினால்
கால்-தொழில் என்று கருதற்க! கையினால்
மேல் தொழிலும் ஆங்கே மிகும்.

194. Ye, the Lord of coastal region where
Waves sway the fronds of Thazhai plant!
Manliness is to do work steadfastly even if harder;
If easier, wouldn't even be done by women?

Jobs easily doable are done by men is not appreciable. Typical manliness is to perform those jobs that are rare to be done. The poem implies that women are prone to do easy work and not capable of doing hard work. In these days of feminism, this is an out-moded idea. Men and women are alike in performing any work of challenge.

இசையாது எனினும், இயற்றி, ஓர் ஆற்றால்
அசையாது, நிற்பதாம் ஆண்மை; இசையுங்கால்,
கண்டல் திரை அலைக்கும் கானல் அம் தண் சேர்ப்ப!
பெண்டிரும் வாழாரோ மற்று?

195. No sense, barring a mere verbal expressions
To say that this caste is good and the other bad;
Since ancientry/real caste is the one consists of
Saintliness, sound education and efforts sincere.

Substance of the poem is that the caste high or low is not meant to be congenitally decided but to be on the basis of meritorious qualities such as eminence, saintliness, education and sincere efforts. Those who possess these qualities alone have to be termed as belonging to higher caste.

> நல்ல குலம் என்றும், தீய குலம் என்றும்,
> சொல் அளவு அல்லால் பொருள் இல்லை; தொல்
> சிறப்பின்
> ஒண் பொருள் ஒன்றோ? தவம், கல்வி, ஆள்வினை,
> என்று இவற்றான் ஆகும், குலம்.

196. Competent men, control the senses and wouldn't
Disclose their efforts until the task achieved;
Under such talented men who scan other's mind
Thro their body movements, the world abides by.

Victory will be achieved by those who make efforts after a strategic study of their enemies. Until they succeed, they won't reveal anything to anybody. But silently they observe the movements of their foes and wait for an occasion to hit their target. To these talented people only, the world is controllable.

> ஆற்றும் துணையும், அறிவினை உள் அடக்கி,
> ஊக்கம் உரையார் உணர்வு உடையார்; ஊக்கம்
> உறுப்பினால் ஆராயும் ஒண்மை உடையார்
> குறிப்பின்கீழ்ப் பட்டது, உலகு.

197. Falling roots like pillar will support
The Banyan tree, partially eaten by white ants;
Similarly infirmity that appears in parent
Will be gotten rid of when sons step in to support.

Implication of the poem is that the young ones of a family should be fully matured and ready to undertake the responsibility from their father. It is their social obligation too.

> சிதலை தினப்பட்ட ஆல மரத்தை,
> மதலை ஆய், மற்று அதன் வீழ் ஊன்றியாங்கு,
> குதலைமை தந்தைகண் தோன்றின், தான் பெற்ற
> புதல்வன் மறைப்ப, கெடும்.

198. There are men as strenuous as a lion of
     Sharp claws and strong hooves even to injure
     The spotted face of elephants; will they ever do
     Disgraceful acts even in their dire poverty at home?

Great men even if fallen on evil days and undergo dire straits at home, will never do anything offensive or humiliating. They will maintain their dignity and propriety.

> ஈனமாய், இல் இருந்து, இன்றி, விளியினும்,
> மானம் தலைவருவ செய்பவோ-யானை
> வரி முகம் புண்படுக்கும் வள் உகிர் நோன் தாள்
> அரிமா மதுகையவர்?

199. Sugar - cane borne flower has solid stem
     And brushy look but has no fragrance;
     So futile if men don't do efforts to perpetuate
     Their name, even if born in great families.

Sugarcane flower will appear white in colour and grown upwards; seemingly as that of flashy white hair on the nape of a horse. But with all that pompous show, it has no flavour. In the same way, even if men are born in great families it is not a criterion. What is expected of them is to make strenuous efforts and achieve things to perpetuate their name and fame in the annals of the world.

தீம் கரும்பு ஈன்ற திரள் கால் உளை அலரி
தேம் கமழ் நாற்றம் இழந்தாஅங்கு, ஓங்கும்
உயர் குடியுள் பிறப்பின் என்னாம்-பெயர் பொறிக்கும்
பேர் ஆண்மை இல்லாக்கடை?

200. Idlers may relish to eat various dishes
Happily offered by Mutharayars but those who dunno
The name of such victuals even earn thro their efforts
The cold liquid rice, which, to them an ambrosia.

Not creditable it is to eat what is offered by Mutharayars and to while away the time in idleness. But the liquid and cold rice earned by poor people is praiseworthy. A simple food earned by one's own efforts is far better than a rich food offered by others. Mutharayars were local chieftains in the period of later Cholas.

பெரு முத்தரையர் பெரிது உவந்து ஈயும்
கருணைச் சோறு ஆர்வர் கயவர்; கருணையப்
பேரும் அறியார், நனி விரும்பு தாளாண்மை
நீரும் அமிழ்து ஆய்விடும்.

ஓ ❖ ❖ ୫୦

Chapter 21 - Shielding of relatives
***

Keeping the relatives in kindness and harmony is a social obligation. There is a separate chapter on this subject in Thirukkural also. This is more important for resourceful people in society because it is they who could offer any help to those who are in need of some assistance or other. Holding relationship with kith and kin is a desirable quality for respectable persons.

201. Pregnant mother forgets birthpangs and
    Delivery pain when looks at the newborn son
    On her lap and likewise, an individual's
    Worries disappear on seeing his own relatives.

All physical sufferings disappear from a pregnant lady, when she observes a newborn male child on her lap after a safe delivery. In the same way, an individual's worries and pains will disappear when his relatives appear closer to him to look after his needs and comforts. The Mother's happiness on a male child is because of the need to have a male member to support the family by hard work and physical labour.

> வயாவும், வருத்தமும், ஈன்றக்கால் நோவும்,
> கவாஅன் மகன் கண்டு தாய் மறந்தாஅங்கு,
> அசாஅத்தான் உற்ற வருத்தம் உசாஅத் தன்
> கேளிரைக் காண, கெடும்.

202. A sprawling tree during hot sun provides
    Cool shade to all who come under its canopy;
    And so useful a fruit - bearing tree also; so
    Duty of a chivalrous male is to serve others.

What is implied here is that a man of genuine love should not mind suffering in the task of helping relatives. He must be ready to bear certain setbacks and problems if only to benefit others.

அழல் மண்டு போழ்தின் அடைந்தவர்கட்கு எல்லாம்
நிழல் மரம்போல் நேர் ஒப்பத் தாங்கி, பழு மரம்போல்
பல்லார் பயன் துய்ப்ப, தான் வருந்தி வாழ்வதே
நல் ஆண்மகற்குக் கடன்.

203. Ye, Lord of several hillocks! No branch of a tree
 Breaks even if to bear solid unripe fruits in plenty
 Greatmen, Likewise would never say "nay'
 From protecting those relatives who seek their help.

Really great men would always be ready to help relatives and those who approach them for help. To illustrate this point, an effective simile is drawn from Nature. No branch of a tree will ever give up bearing the fruits grown in. Similarly great men too bear such heavy and responsible work of safeguarding relatives and friends.

அடுக்கல் மலை நாட! தற் சேர்ந்தவரை
எடுக்கலம் என்னார் பெரியோர்;-அடுத்து அடுத்து
வன் காய் பலபல காய்ப்பினும், இல்லையே,
தன் காய் பொறுக்கலாக் கொம்பு?

204. Friendship with loafers however close it's in
 Worldly sense, would last for a few days; but of
 Intimacy with faultless men of virtues would be
 As solid as that of their firmness to earn spirituality.

Friendship with low-persons wouldn't last long for more than a few days. But intimacy with genuine great men would be static. In other words, that intimacy will be as strong and firm as that of the great men's efforts to attain spirituality.

உலகு அறியத் தீரக் கலப்பினும், நில்லா,
சில பகல் ஆம், சிற்றினத்தார் கேண்மை; நிலை திரியா-
நிற்கும் பெரியோர் நெறி அடைய நின்றனைத்தால்,
ஒற்கம் இலாளர் தொடர்பு.

205. Wiping off even prodigal's poverty and possess
     A noble quality of never saying at all, phrases such as
     He is such, 'he is my relative', he is different' is the
     One who is entitled to be the greatest of all.

The greatest man is one who does not discriminate good from the bad or known from the unknown but indiscriminately extending help to all those who are in need of it. He alone is entitled to be called as the greatest of all whom I know.

'இன்னர்; இனையர்; எமர்; பிறர்' என்னும் சொல்
என்னும் இலர் ஆம் இயல்பினால் துன்னி,
தொலை மக்கள் துன்பம் தீர்ப்பாரே,-யார்மாட்டும்
தலைமக்கள் ஆகற்பாலர்.

206. More tasty it's to drink even rice-gruel with no salt
     Offered in any vessel by endearing kindred
     Than eating cooked rice as white as tiger's claw
     From undesirables in a pot with sugary milk.

Genuine love is desirable; hatred is detestable, This point is explained with illustration. Food unpalatable from a kind hearted person is better than a tasty food from the hands of an undesirable man.

பொற் கலத்துப் பெய்த புலி உகிர் வான் புழுக்கல்
அக்காரம் பாலோடு அமரார் கைத்து உண்டலின்,
உப்பு இலிப் புற்கை, உயிர்போல் கிளைஞர் மாட்டு
எக் கலத்தானும் இனிது.

207. Ye! Listen my Lord! Even if food oven - fresh
     Offered on time as lunch by cheerless relatives
     Bitter like neem-seed but by relatives in late hour
     Even if it's mere leaves boiled, tasty it will be!

Even if palatable ghee - rice is offered by unfriendly relatives, it will be as bitter as neem - seed, But even if mere boiled greenleaves are offered by hospitable relatives, it would be highly agreeable and tasty to the guests.

> நாள்வாய்ப் பெறினும், தம் நள்ளாதார் இல்லத்து,
> வேளாண்மை வெங் கருனை வேம்பு ஆகும்; கேளாய்;
> அபரானப் போழ்தின் அடகு இடுவரேனும்,
> தமர் ஆயார்மாட்டே இனிது.

208. Those who, as anvil in smithy repeatedly eat
In one's house may belie him ungratefully
Like tongs in fire but genuine relatives would be
Like iron rod gets into fire along with gadgets.

A metaphor is drawn from smithy in this poetic passage. The act of repeated hammering of iron gadgets on the anvil is compared to the act of repeated eating in one's house. Tongs will go into the fire with gadgets and come back at once. This is purported to indicate the friends who are not fully reliable. But iron rod goes with the gadget into fire and remain there until the purpose is served. So iron rods are compared to faithful relatives who are always standing by their kinsmen in the ups and downs of earthy life.

> முட்டிகை போல முனியாது, வைகலும்,
> கொட்டி உண்பாரும், குறுடுபோல் கைவிடுவர்,
> சுட்டுக்கோல் போல, எரியும் புகுவரே,
> நட்டார் எனப்படுவார்.

209. Ye, Lady of a garland of fragrant flowers!
                                    Relatives
who share happiness with kindred but share not
                                             their
Sufferings too as if their own until their last, what
                                              else
Is for them to do good in the next birth?

Whatever good the resourceful relatives are meant to do, be in happiness or in misery, they should do to their near and dear in this birth itself. It is their duty. Planning or promising such good deeds to one's own relatives in the next birth is rather untenable and impractical. Even though many poems of this anthology speaks firmly of next birth, here this stanza doesn't give credence to an after-life.

> நறு மலர்த் தண் கோதாய்! நட்டார்க்கு நட்டார்
> மறுமையும் செய்வது ஒன்று உண்டோ-இறும் அளவும்,
> இன்புறுவ இன்புற்று எழீஇ, அவரொடு
> துன்புறுவ துன்புறாக்கால்?

210. Eating even an oven-fresh roasted dish
 Is like neem seeds in the houses of loveless men;
 But even watery gruel of rice in the homes of loving
 Relatives is like wholesomely delicious manna.

Neem seeds are bitter in taste. Even a nicely prepared dish offered unpleasantly, is like eating neem seeds; but liquid diet like gruel will be like a tasty food when it is offered with love and affection.

> விருப்பு இலார் இல்லத்து வேறு இருந்து உண்ணும்
> வெருக்குக் கண் வெங்கருனை வேம்பு ஆம்; விருப்புடைத்
> தன் போல்வார் இல்லுள் தயங்கு நீர்த் தண் புற்கை
> என்போடு இயைந்த அமிழ்து.

Chapter 22 - Study of Friendship
***

One may get acquainted with anybody and move with him informally. But friendship and intimacy are of deeper significance. One should think twice before holding intimacy. A study of the man and his qualities therefore have to be observed before moving friendly with him. This is what this chapter delineate.

211. Intimacy for ever the thoughtful, well learned of
     Scholars is like tasting sugarcane from top
     To bottom but contact with persons unqualified
     Is like tasting it from bottom to the top.

Friendship with learned scholars will be tasty, tastier and, even the tastiest as that of chewing sugarcane from top to bottom; but contact with that of average persons will be like tasting sugarcane from bottom to the top.

கருத்து உணர்ந்து கற்று அறிந்தார் கேண்மை, எஞ்
ஞான்றும்,
குருத்தின் கரும்பு தின்றற்றே; குருத்திற்கு
எதிர் செலத் தின்றன்ன தகைத்துஅரோ, என்றும்
மதுரம் இலாளர் தொடர்பு.

212. Ye, the Lord of hilly country where birds flee
     On the roaring sound of cascade! to hold intimacy
     One should gauge one's birth in a group
     Rather than studying one's own mind.

What is implied here is that birth and parentage are the criteria to determine the deep and unwavering friendship of a person. Study of his mind before deciding his friendship will not be as strong and valid as the study of one's own hereditary link, family and parentage. The poet affirms the genetic influence on one's own character and behaviour.

> இற் பிறப்பு எண்ணி, இடை திரியார் என்பது ஓர்
> நல் புடை கொண்டமை அல்லது,-பொன் கேழ்
> புனல் ஒழுகப் புள் இரியும் பூங் குன்ற நாட!-
> மனம் அறியப்பட்டது ஒன்று அன்று.

213. Even if known well, elephant in rut or anger
    Kills its mahout but even if spear thrown in its body
    Dog will wag its tail and so keep friendship
    With those like dog and not like elephants.

Despite grooming by a mahout, an elephant will not spare him if it gets rut or angry on some reason or other. But a dog even if wounded by its master in a fury would faithfully wag its tail. Friends of such exceptional love like that of a dog, one should hold and not that of an elephant that is vengeful.

> யானை அனையவர் நண்பு ஒரீஇ, நாய் அனையார்
> கேண்மை கெழீஇக் கொளல்வேண்டும்;-யானை
> அறிந்து அறிந்தும், பாகனையே கொல்லும்; எறிந்த வேல்
> மெய்யதா, வால் குழைக்கும், நாய்.

214. Great men wouldn't hold friendship with those
    Who live nearer for long time but inharmonious;
    But is there anybody given up genuine intimacy
    Even though they are away for a long time?

No. Great men would not give up the genuine intimacy of real friends, even though they are separated and away for a long time. But they would not approve of and align with certain others who are living close by but not amicable.

> பல நாளும் பக்கத்தார் ஆயினும், நெஞ்சில்
> சில நாளும் ஒட்டாரோடு ஒட்டார்; பல நாளும்
> நீத்தார் என, கைவிடல் உண்டோ-தம் நெஞ்சத்து
> யாத்தாரோடு யாத்த தொடர்பு?

215. Friendship real is like a blossomed flower
That never closes its petal on a branch of tree;
Those lovely as pond-flower but shirk their face
Neither are liked nor or they held in friendship.

Flowers that blossom on the branches of trees never close their petals; as cheerful as they began. This is compared to a real friendship that never changes but remains constant. Aquatic flowers in a tank blossom in the morning and close their petals in the evening. This closure of petals is compared to the shirking of one's face. Such a person of shirking face is not fit for friendship. Similies, drawn from nature indicate how far ancient Tamil poets have closely observed its various aspects.

> கோட்டுப்பூப் போல மலர்ந்து, பின் கூம்பாது,
> வேட்டதே வேட்டது ஆம் நட்பு ஆட்சி; தோட்ட
> கயப்பூப்போல் முன் மலர்ந்து, பின் கூம்புவாரை
> நயப்பாரும் நட்பாரும் இல்.

216. Lowest of friends are alike arecanut tree
Those of mediocre are alike coconut tree
Highest of friends are alike Palmyra tree
And their intimacy will be as such unchangeable.

Arecanut plant has to be watered regularly and if not it will fade. Similarly friends of the last category shall be obliged to their satisfaction; otherwise they will never be our friends. Coconut trees may be watered off and on; and so also their friendship. Palmyra, once sowed on a piece of wet ground will grow of its own until it yields at a later time. Friends of the highest level are therefore compared to Palmyra trees. Without expecting anything in return, they try to help us.

> கடையாயார் நட்பில் கமுகு அனையர்; ஏனை
> இடையாயார் தெங்கின் அனையர்; தலையாயார்
> எண்ண அரும் பெண்ணை போன்று, இட்ட ஞான்று
>   இட்டதே,
> தொன்மை உடையார் தொடர்பு.

217. Though a black leafy dish cooked in used water
If given courteously, is like manna; but if by
A person discourteous, even a pure white rice
Dainty, delicious with side – dish is alike *Ettikkaai*.

Sweet it is even if a simple, poor edible is given by the host with courtesy and kindness. If offered inharmoniously even if it is a delicious rice food, it is as bitter and unpalatable as *Ettikkaai*. Implication is that one is meant to choose benevolent and good people as friends.

கழுநீருள் கார் அடகேனும், ஒருவன்
விழுமிதாக் கொள்ளின் அமிழ்து ஆம்; விழுமிய
குய்த் துவை ஆர் வெண் சோறே ஆயினும், மேவாதார்
கைத்துண்டல் காஞ்சிரங்காய்.

218. What else of intimacy if not helpful even if
As minuscule as flea's leg, despite closer to us
As paws of the dogs are; so grapple the
Intimacy of those who are broader in love as canals.

Friendship of those who are in no way helpful even in emergency is of no use. This is like a proverbial expression that' a friend in need is a friend indeed. Hence it is counseled that persons of helping tendency may be chosen as friends.

நாய்க் கால் சிறு விரல்போல் நன்கு அணியர் ஆயினும்,
ஈக் கால் துணையும் உதவாதார் நட்பு என்னாம்?
சேய்த்தானும் சென்று கொளல்வேண்டும், செய்
                               விளைக்கும்
வாய்க்கால் அனையார் தொடர்பு.

219. Enmity is better than amity with unwise men
Death is blessed to disease incurable;
Killing a man is higher than humiliating him
Reviling is better than adoring a man unworthy.

The second line of the poem seems to be advocating Euthanasia or mercy killing. But who to propose it and who to do it is a question. Thomas More, in his *'Utopia'* champions the cause of euthanasia. A few countries have legally approved it in the rarest of rare cases but many countries including India have not.

> தெளிவு இலார் நட்பின் பகை நன்று; சாதல்
> விளியா அரு நோயின் நன்றால்; அளிய
> இகழ்தலின் கோறல் இனிதே; மற்று இல்ல
> புகழ்தலின் வைதலே நன்று.

220. Friendship with a deadly snake may even
 Be grieving when parting away from it;
 Hence move and compare for days on end
 With many and hold only the deserving as friends.

Holding even familiarity rather than friendship with reptiles such as snake is very strange, odd and unusual excepting to the snake - charmers. Perhaps to insist on the point taken up, the poet has overlooked the pragmatic side of life.

> மரீஇ, பலரொடு பல் நாள் முயங்கி,
> பொரீஇ, பொருள்தக்கார்க் கோடலே வேண்டும்;
> பரீஇ, உயிர் செகுக்கும் பாம்பொடும் இன்னா,
> மரீஇ,இப், பின்னைப் பிரிவு.

ಲ‍ೆ ♦ ❖ ♦ ಐ

Chapter 23 - Forbearance
***

This is a quality of toleration, patience, self-control and a willingness to forgive those who have knowingly or unknowingly offended us.

221. Those whom we deemed the friendliest
     Have to be borne with, even if they offend;
     Paddy has chaff and water has its froth
     Even the soft flower has also its outer - petal.

No one is free from some setback or fault. But these stigmas or faults should not be aggravated or exaggerated. Once a friendship is cultivated with a person, and if that person has offended us for some reason or other, that should be forgotten. This is the main theme of this entire chapter.

>நல்லார் எனத் தாம் நனி விரும்பிக் கொண்டாரை,
>அல்லார் எனினும், அடக்கிக் கொளல்வேண்டும்;
>நெல்லுக்கு உமி உண்டு; நீர்க்கு நுரை உண்டு;
>புல் இதழ் பூவிற்கும் உண்டு.

222. Even if water breaches repeatedly despite
     Barriers, peasants continue to barricade it with
     No fury and likewise, if friends of our choice do
     Hateful offences, they have to be borne with.

Any farmer will try to put a build across the small streams to direct water into the fields. If water overflows or break the land, the farmer will never be angry with water.

>செறுத்தோறு உடைப்பினும், செம் புனலோடு ஊடார்,
>மறுத்தும் சிறைசெய்வர், நீர் நசைஇ வாழ்நர்;-
>வெறுப்ப வெறுப்பச் செயினும், பொறுப்பரே,
>தாம் வேண்டிக் கொண்டார் தொடர்பு.

223. Ye, the Lord of hillocks where lovely bees
Hum around bright kongu flowers! Forbearance
Of one ensures friendship of two and hence
If a friend is deeply offensive, isn't it right to forbear?

The poet desires that one of the two friends has to necessarily observe toleration so that the friendship of the two will survive. If not, the much-earned friendship will get spoiled. This is a kind of two-in-one in the world of friendliness. Kongu is a tropical tree well known for its timber,

> இறப்பவே தீய செயினும், தன் நட்டார்
> பொறுத்தல் தகுவது ஒன்று அன்றோ?-நிறக் கோங்கு
> உருவ வண்டு ஆர்க்கும் உயர் வரை நாட!-
> ஒருவர் பொறை இருவர் நட்பு.

224. Ye! Lord of a coast where boats side – ways
Pearls cast on shores by warring waves;
If close friends are incorrigibly bad, their
Friendship is like fire to burn the heart.

Offence if committed once or twice by close friends, it can be tolerated. If such friends continue to be offensive and inharmonious, their behavior is like fire to burn our heart. The reason is neither we can easily set aside a friend of olden days nor we can bear with continuous lapses or misdeeds.

> மடி திரை தந்திட்ட வான் கதிர் முத்தம்
> கடு விசை நாவாய் கரை அலைக்கும் சேர்ப்ப!
> விடுதற்கு அரியார் இயல்பு இலரேல், நெஞ்சம்
> சுடுதற்கு மூட்டிய தீ.

225. We make fire at home deliberately to make use of
Even though fire is known to be destructible;
And as such, even if they do harm, we have to
Keep dissociable men also as we hold gold at home!

Fire destroys and ruins. But still we make use of it for benevolent purposes such as cooking and warming ourselves. In the same way, if certain friends behave erratically, we have to bear with them for some time and then make better use of them. It is like one who keeps himself neither nearer to nor far away from fire.

> இன்னா செயினும், விடற்பாலர் அல்லாரைப்
> பொன்னாகப் போற்றிக் கொளல் வேண்டும்-பொன்னொடு
> நல் இல் சிதைத்த தீ நாள்தொறும் நாடித் தம்
> இல்லத்தில் ஆக்குதலால்.

226. Ye, Lord of the hill of lofty height and of
     Bamboos sky-high! Will there be anybody
     Cutting his finger for it having hit his eye?
     So its improper to give up dissociable friend

If close friends behave erroneously sometimes, they need not be given up; as much as we do not cut our finger if it hurts the eye unwittingly. Therefore better not to part with any of our friends because of some error occasionally on any one of them.

> இன்னா செயினும், விடுதற்கு அரியாரைத்
> துன்னாத் துறத்தல் தகுவதோ? துன்னு அருஞ்சீர்
> விண் குத்தும் நீள் வரை வெற்ப!- களைபவோ,
> கண் குத்திற்று என்று தம் கை?

227. Ye! Lord of a pleasant coast! Even if evil is
     Done by a friend, great men won't expostulate!
     Once befriended, if his offences are exaggerated,
     Those weak - minded are lower than the offenders.

Men of forbearance are strong-willed and those who are not but go on exaggerating the evils or blunders of friends are, in a way are not only weak - minded but lower in calibre than the offenders. Forbearance is thus affirmed as a virtue.

இலங்கு நீர்த் தண் சேர்ப்ப! இன்னா செயினும்,
கலந்து பழி காணார், சான்றோர்; கலந்தபின்,
தீமை எடுத்து உரைக்கும் திண் அறிவு இல்லாதார்
தாழும், அவரின் கடை.

228. Ye, Lord of the land of resounding cascade!
When other's evil on us is perused, it's found
To have been destined, what else to worry
In our mind, the offences of close friends!

When close friends offend us, we should not take it to heart and feel sorry for it, even evils committed by others are taken in and attributed to destiny.

ஏதிலார் செய்தது இறப்பவே தீது எனினும்,
நோதக்கது என் உண்டாம், நோக்குங்கால்? காதல்
கழுமியார் செய்த,-கறங்கு அருவி நாட!
விழுமிதாம், நெஞ்சத்துள் நின்று.

229. If those who were our friends earlier
Are found to be unfriendly at present
Let us still respect them more than of our friends
By concealing their unfriendliness with ourselves.

Great men are expected not to reveal faithless or unfriendly activities of those who were our close friends once though not at present. The Tamil original has a rhetorical flourish of having used one and the same word for four times in this poem.

தமர் என்று தாம் கொள்ளப்பட்டவர் தம்மைத்
தமர் அன்மை தாம் அறிந்தார் ஆயின், அவரைத்
தமரினும் நன்கு மதித்து, தமர் அன்மை
தம்முள் அடக்கிக்கொளல்!

230. If I wander about studying merits and defects
Of once a befriended one, let me go with the
         mockery
Of people to hell where go men who didn't guard
The secrets of a close friend of theirs.

Forbearance of offences committed by friends is thus reinforced by the poet himself. Before fixing a man as friend, his vices and virtues ought to have been studied. Having deeply cultivated friendship with him and then begin studying his qualities is almost like a sin. More so, if any secret of the said person is revealed further.

> 'குற்றமும், ஏனைக் குணமும், ஒருவனை
> நட்டபின் நாடித் திரிவேனேல், நட்டான்
> மறை காவா விட்டவன் செல்வுழிச் செல்க,
> அறை கடல் சூழ் வையம் நக!'

Chapter 24 - Undesirable intimacy
***

This chapter speaks about the hypocrisy of those who pretend to have a genuine and better friendship than they actually have. So it behoves us to go in for choosing a right person as friend. Avoidance of bad elements is one of the ways to fix a good friend. This is what the following ten poems attempt to elucidate.

231. Ye! Lord of the dark hilly country of Cascades !
    Until their purpose is fulfilled, many will remain
    In our hut of threadbare ceiling for drawing out
    And holding rain water in vessels and barricading
    with mud.

A few persons would not mind remaining with us even in a dilapidated hut until they obtain our help. They disappear. They are opportunists but not friends. Beware of them, the poet says. Friendship for a wilful purpose is brought out by the metaphor of an old cottage with a thatch threadbare.

> செறிப்பு இல் பழங் கூரைச் சேறு அணை ஆக
> இறைத்தும், நீர் ஏற்றும், கிடப்பர்,-கறைக் குன்றம்
> பொங்கு அருவி தாழும் புனல் வரை நல் நாட!
> தம் கருமம் முற்றும் துணை.

232. Ye, the Lord of cascades! Friendship of great men
    Is highly beneficial as much as seasonal rains;
    But of those who are illbred not great is as useless
    As the rainless days of drought.

Great men of real friendship will be extending help without expecting anything in return. But of others will be very particular in getting help only but no help to others at all. This category is meant to be avoided because it is not suitable for friendship.

சீரியார் கேண்மை சிறந்த சிறப்பிற்று ஆய்,
மாரிபோல் மாண்ட பயத்தது ஆம்; மாரி
வறந்தக்கால் போலுமே,-வால் அருவி நாட!
சிறந்தக்கால் சீர் இலார் நட்பு.

233. Enjoining camaraderie of excellent thinkers
Is like a paradisical pleasure, a likeable event;
Mixing with useless persons of no knowledge of books
Is like one of the miseries of hellish life.

One's contact with scholarly men is always refreshing, cheerful and informative; but of unlettered is inactive, dull and lethargic. Hence such a contact is undesirable.

நுண் உணர்வினாரொடு கூடி நுகர்வு உடைமை
விண்ணுலகே ஒக்கும் விழைவிற்றால்; நுண் நூல்
உணர்வு இலர் ஆகிய ஊதியம் இல்லார்ப்
புணர்தல் நிரயத்துள் ஒன்று.

234. Ye Lord of hills surrounded by sandal groves!"
As fire in straw appears to grow raging but get
Put out soon, friendship of loveless men appears
To grow well but get mitigated, and extinguished.

Implication is that such a meaningless friendship may be given up instead of clinging on to.

பெருகுவது போலத் தோன்றி, வைத் தீப்போல்
ஒருபொழுதும் செல்லாதே நந்தும்,-அருகு எல்லாம்
சந்தன நீள் சோலைச் சாரல் மலை நாட!
பந்தம் இலாளர் தொடர்பு.

235. To say 'we could do' even impossible tasks and
To delay inordinate, the achievable things, are the
Qualities that would render unhappy even the saints
Who would normally, maintain a cool composure.

Saints will objectively be normal in temperament – neither happy nor unhappy. Such saints too will be unhappy at the boasting and delaying tactics of certain abnormal persons. The poem purports to say that such persons are not desirable to be in friendliness.

> 'செய்யாத செய்தும் நாம்' என்றலும், செய்வதனைச்
> செய்யாது தாழ்த்துக்கொண்டு ஓட்டலும், மெய்யாக
> இன்புறூஉம் பெற்றி இகழ்ந்தார்க்கும், அந் நிலையே
> துன்புறூஉம் பெற்றி தரும்.

236. Though born of one water - shed and grown up
 Together, Aambal flower will not be equal to
 Kuvalai;
 Likewise, men of unpleasant qualities, despite
 friendly
 With great men, will be lower and different in
 calibre.

Men of ignoble qualities will be lower in calibre even if they are associated with great and virtuous men. This point is explained by a comparison of two aquatic flowers. *Aambal* flower is lesser than *Kuvalai* in fragrance, colour and blossoming.

> ஒரு நீர்ப் பிறந்து, ஒருங்கு நீண்டக்கடைத்தும்,
> விரி நீர்க் குவளையை ஆம்பல் ஒக்கல்லா;-
> பெரு நீரார் கேண்மை கொளினும், நீர் அல்லார்
> கருமங்கள் வேறுபடும்.

237. Ye, Lord of a hill where young she - monkeys
 Playfully punched on and plucked things from their
 Fathers, with fingers as slender as dried pods!
 Friendship with disagreeable men is undesirable.

Like – mindedness is a basic pre – requisite for an effective friendship. If there is no such harmony, better it is to avoid it. The last sentence is the cream of the passage. The remaining three is purported to have addressed to the Lord of a hilly country. Wildlife habit of monkeys is pictured therein.

> முற்றல் சிறு மந்தி முற்பட்ட தந்தையை
> நெற்றுக் கண்டன்ன விரலால் ஞெமிர்த்திட்டுக்
> குற்றிப் பறிக்கும் மலை நாட! இன்னாதே,
> ஒற்றுமை கொள்ளாதார் நட்பு.

238. If not pledging my rare life to a friend's
 Speedy rescue of his misery, let me go with
 World's insult to hell to which go the one
 Who outraged the modesty of his friend's wife.

This is almost like an oath - taking that the proponent accursed to go to hell, if he doesn't go to rescue his friend from a misery. In other words, genuine friends should speedily help their friends, if they are in distress.

> முட்டு உற்ற போழ்தில் முடுகி, என் ஆர் உயிரை
> நட்டான் ஒருவன் கை நீட்டேனேல், நட்டான்
> கடி மனை கட்டு அழித்தான் செல்வுழிச் செல்க!
> நெடுமொழி வையம் நக!

239. Ye, Lord of a hill, famous for honey!
 Befriending with ill – informed low-bred after
 Giving up intimacy with well – informed great men
 Is like replacing cow's ghee by neem oil in a vessel.

Friendship with sweet and gentle–natured persons is always desirable but not the association with low - level men. Ghee is compared to a benevolent friendship and neem oil is to the familiarity of loafers.

> ஆன் படுநெய் பெய் கலனுள் அது களைந்து,
> வேம்பு அடு நெய் பெய்தனைத்துஅரோ-தேம் படு
> நல் வரை நாட!-நயம் உணர்வார் நண்பு ஒரீஇ,
> புல்லறிவினாரொடு நட்பு.

240. Absence of governance in an administrator
   Is like adulteration of drinkable milk with water;
   Similarly well – informed men mingling with loafers
   Is like cobra killing itself in copulating with virian snake.

If a ruler is found to be incapable of administering his territory, perhaps he is a misfit or unfit. The poet says that the ruler's incapacity is like mere water added to milk – no use. So also useless if a learned man keeps himself in friendliness with lazy and inactive fellows. The veracity of the last line of the stanza is not vouch safed by any zoologist. Even, statements apocryphal are taken in by poets to mobilize their points. It may be recalled that Shakespeare in *As you like it* says that lions would not kill any man if he is found to be sleeping. Who to say that it is true?

உருவிற்கு அமைந்தான்கண் ஊராண்மை இன்மை,
பருகற்கு அமைந்தபால் நீர் அளாயற்றே;
தெரிவு உடையார் தீஇனத்தர் ஆகுதல், நாகம்
விரி பெடையோடு ஆடி, விட்டற்று.

ಃ ❖ ❖ ೞ

Chapter – 25 Knowledge
***

Truly speaking, knowledge is an awareness of anything and everything. It is expandable and limitless. That is why, Tennyson says that

"Knowledge is like a sinking star
Beyond the utmost bound of human thought"

Following ten stanzas concentrate on one's own distinctive awareness of which is deserving friendship and which is not.

241. Strong and divine Raghu, the planet wouldn't
 Go to eclipse crescent moon and strong men too
 Would deem it a shame to confront when
 Their enemies are in low - spirit and weak.

It is a shame for a chivalrous and real hero to defeat an enemy when he is miserably a weakling. Hence he would not attack his adversary. The poet implies that to hurt a weak enemy is rather a shameful activity. A hero to establish his honour has to fight against a competent enemy. *Raghu* and *Kedu* refer the moon's ascending and descending node. Referring them as snakes attempting to swallow the moon is actually known as the lunar eclipse.

> பகைவர் பணிவு இடம் நோக்கி, தகவு உடையார்
> தாமேயும் நாணித் தலைச்செல்லார்;-காணாய்;
> இளம் பிறை ஆயக்கால் திங்களைச் சேராது,
> அணங்கு அருந் துப்பின் அரா.

242. Ye, Lord of a cool coastal region! Humbleness is
 An ornament for men of poverty but if he behaves
 Exceedingly with no restraint, his own group
 Will be reproached as low by the people of his place.

If a man suffers from poverty, he must make himself humble and low; then only the other resourceful persons will come forward to help him. If he behaves overbearingly, nobody will be sympathetic and helpful to him.

> நளி கடல் தண் சேர்ப்ப! நல்கூர்ந்த மக்கட்கு
> அணிகலம் ஆவது அடக்கம்; பணிவு இல் சீர்
> மாத்திரை இன்றி நடக்குமேல், வாழும் ஊர்
> கோத்திரம் கூறப்படும்.

243. In whatever land you sow a seed, no *Kanjiram*
　　 Will ever be a coconut sapling; Southerners
　　 May attain paradise while Northerners
　　 Haven't as heavenly pleasure is through efforts.

An opinion that prevailed in olden days was that heavenly pleasure is obtainable only to the northerners but not to the Southerners of India. This poem rejects that notion and makes it clear that the celestial pleasure is more out of benevolent efforts and not out of the locality that one belongs. Southern part of India was deemed to be the land of *Rakshashas* in olden days and hence the refusal of it in this poem.

> எந் நிலத்து வித்து இடினும், காஞ்சிரங் காழ் தெங்கு ஆகா;
> தென் நாட்டவரும் சுவர்க்கம் புகுதலால்,
> தன்னால்தான் ஆகும் மறுமை; வட திசையும்,
> கொன்னாளர் சாலப் பலர்.

244. Banana never changes its sweetness even
　　 If it's ripened amidst neem leaves and
　　 As such, even if company is bad, the friendship
　　 Of virtuous people will never go stale and harmful.

Really good – minded people shall never allow their mind spoiled even if they had to keep company with undesirable persons. Better not to align with them at all is implied.

வேம்பின் இலையுள் கனியினும், வாழை தன்
தீம் சுவை யாதும் திரியாதாம்; ஆங்கே,
இனம் தீது எனினும், இயல்பு உடையார் கேண்மை
மனம் தீது ஆம் பக்கம் அரிது.

245. Ye, Lord of a cool coastal region! Tasty water
　　　Arises adjacent to sea as salty water
　　　Next to hill and as such, men will not be identical
　　　To the group they belong but to character they possess.

Men are bound to get their character changed because of company. But if they are strong in conviction and firm in thinking, their benevolent virtues will never change. What the stanza implies is that even if any man falls into a bad company, he must cultivate a determination to uphold his virtuous character.

கடல் சார்ந்தும் இன் நீர் பிறக்கும்; மலை சார்ந்தும்
உப்பு ஈண்டு உவரி பிறத்தலால், தம்தம்
இனத்து அனையர் அல்லர்-எறி கடல் தண் சேர்ப்ப!
மனத்து அனையர், மக்கள் என்பார்.

246. Ye, Lord of a sea coast of huge *Punnai* trees!
　　　Will noble minded men ever be attaching once
　　　And detaching then from friendly people?
　　　Wise and better it's than to be waywardly like that!

Once befriended with somebody and then withdrawing from him is rather painful. So, better it is to choose a person only after finding out his good qualities.

பராஅரைப் புன்னை படு கடல் தண் சேர்ப்ப!
ஒராஅலும் ஒட்டலும் செய்பவோ, நல்ல
மருஉச் செய்து யார்மாட்டும் தங்கும் மனத்தார்
விராஅஅய்ச் செய்யாமை நன்று.

247. Pleasure it is to befriend erudite men who
    Measures what we have in our mind; to join with
    The unwise who cannot understand even
    Our explicit views, is rather a distress.

What has been explained in the previous stanza is repeated in a different version.

> உணர உணரும் உணர்வு உடையாரைப்
> புணர, புணருமாம் இன்பம்; புணரின்
> தெரியத் தெரியும் தெரிவு இலாதாரைப்
> பிரிய, பிரியுமாம் நோய்.

248. One who fixes himself in good condition
    Gets dislocated to fall down fathoms deep
    Goes on raising his status from stage to stage and
    Arranges to be on top is none other than himself.

Four different stages of a man's status are listed out in the stanza. It goes without saying that it is the man who is responsible either to chart out his course of life or to fall down or to raise his status gradually and at length to be on the top level of life. It is his knowledge that must direct him suitably.

> நல் நிலைக்கண் தன்னை நிறுப்பானும், தன்னை
> நிலை கலக்கிக் கீழ் இடுவானும், நிலையினும்
> மேல்மேல் உயர்த்து நிறுப்பானும், தன்னைத்
> தலையாகச் செய்வானும், தான்.

249. Ye! Lord of waves roaring coastline!
    To get the purpose served, great men
    Rarely goes behind the unwise persons
    Is not idiocy but an essential timely wiseness.

The last line of the Tamil original, as it is, is meant as explained in the English version above. But Chemboor Vidwan Arumugam Servai in his voluminous commentary of Naladiyar transposed the last three words and interprets that goes behind illiterate persons is "unwise and low".

> கரும வரிசையால், கல்லாதார் பின்னும்
> பெருமை உடையாரும் சேறல்,-அரு மரபின்
> ஓதம் அறற்றும் ஒலி கடல் தண் சேர்ப்ப!
> பேதைமை அன்று; அது அறிவு.

250. If only possible, to do all benevolent things plus
 Enjoying its benefits and extending
 All charities to deserving virtuous persons
 Is like a ship safely arrived with merchandise.

Such a person who does all these husbandries in his family life is a man of wiseness. He is indirectly compared to a ship that has safely arrived the inland harbour with all the merchandise gathered from various lands afar.

> கருமமும் உள்படா, போகமும் துவ்வா,
> தருமமும் தக்கார்க்கே செய்யா, ஒருநிலையே
> முட்டு இன்றி மூன்றும் முடியுமேல், அஃது என்ப,
> 'பட்டினம் பெற்ற கலம்.'

☙ ♦ ❖ ♦ ❧

Chapter 26 - Irrationalism
***

Not possessing the extra ordinary capacity of discriminating good from bad is irrationalism. Knowledge with ability is a part of rationalistic quality.

251. Devoid of excellent knowledge is poverty and
     Its possession, a fabulous wealth and to think deeply
     Even a hermaphrodite, with a loss of masculinity
     Wears herself a high enticing set of jewels...

Female eunuch may even decorate herself with a lot of gorgeous jewels but it doesn't make her beautiful. In the same way, what the poem explicitly says is that if unintelligent and irrationalistic persons possess wealth, it won't give them any recognition in society. It is only the knowledge that makes a person rich and resourceful.

நுண் உணர்வு இன்மை வறுமை; அஃது உடைமை
பண்ணப் பணைத்த பெருஞ் செல்வம்;-எண்ணுங்கால்,
பெண் அவாய், ஆண் இழந்த பேடி அணியாளோ,
கண் அவாத் தக்க கலம்?

252. Be aware why scholars of versatility suffer
     With their eminence tilted; it's due to their link
     With Goddess of knowledge, the Goddess of wealth
     Wouldn't favour them out of her feigned dislike.

Traditional belief is that eminent intellectual persons will be suffering for want of material wealth. This is not to think of them lower than others. But the reason is according to the poet, wherever Saraswathi, the goddess of learning is, Lakshmi, the Goddess of wealth wouldn't remain to favour him. That means both the female deities do not see eye to eye; wherever the one is, the other one won't step in.

> பல் ஆன்ற கேள்விப் பயன் உணர்வார் பாடு அழிந்து,
> அல்லல் உழப்பது அறிதிரேல்,-தொல் சிறப்பின்
> நாவின் கிழத்தி உறைதலால், சேராளே,
> பூவின் கிழத்தி புலந்து.

253. One who neglected and spurned a father's
 Counsel to learn will feel disgraced with
 Shame, if a written script is shown to him for
 Reading it in an assemblage of many persons.

His illiteracy will betray his ignorance and he will nicely withdraw from the place without reading the written script.

> 'கல்' என்று தந்தை கழற, அதனை ஓர்
> சொல் என்று கொள்ளாது இகழ்ந்தவன், மெல்ல
> எழுத்து ஓலை பல்லார்முன் நீட்ட, விளியா,
> வழுக் கோலைக் கொண்டுவிடும்.

254. Even if a robust illiterate slowly gets in
 And sits amidst wisemen, it's like
 Ensconcing of a dog, even if he incoherently
 Blabbers, it is like the barking of a cur.

Illiterate and unwise men are not qualified to sit amidst wisemen and confabulate in the assembly. To explicitly speak low of the illiterates, the poet has compared them to dogs.

> கல்லாது நீண்ட ஒருவன், உலகத்து,
> நல்லறிவாளரிடைப் புக்கு, மெல்ல
> இருப்பினும், நாய் இருந்தற்றே; இராஅது
> உரைப்பினும், நாய் குரைத்தற்று.

255. Men of low calibre get into ill-qualified persons
 And narrate what they haven't learnt;
 But learned, being aware of their hollowness
 Wouldn't say anything distinctly even if asked.

It is not a matter of pride if uneducated persons flaunt their ill – equipped little knowledge to a crowd of semi-literates. Educated persons maintain laconic brevity in communicating with others.

> புல்லாப் புன் கோட்டிப் புலவரிடைப் புக்கு,
> கல்லாத சொல்லும், கடை எல்லாம்; கற்ற
> கடாஅயினும் சான்றவர் சொல்லார், பொருள்மேல்
> படாஅ விடுபாக்கு அறிந்து.

256. Well qualified scholars cautiously speak
 Fearing lapses but others are vociferous
 Unmindfully and this is like clattering of
 Dry palm leaves against green leaves of no sound.

What the poem implies is that it is unwise to speak excessively without any basis of reason and thought.

> கற்று அறிந்த நாவினார் சொல்லார், தம் சோர்வு அஞ்சி
> மற்றையர் ஆவார் பகர்வர்;-பனையின்மேல்
> வற்றிய ஓலை கலகலக்கும்; எஞ் ஞான்றும்
> பச்சோலைக்கு இல்லை, ஒலி.

257. Preaching of ethical ways to ignorant public
 Won't reach their ears as a peg doesn't get planted
 On a rocky hill and it is like pouring of
 Mango juice in a wooden trough meant for pigs.

It is unwise to preach benevolent ideas to idiotic persons. This need not be taken as a hard and fast rule. Even if that unwise person is genuinely willing to listen and follow the ideas, any amount of counselling may be done to him. It may be recalled that *"Discretion is the better part of Valour"*

> பன்றிக் கூழ்ப் பத்தரில் தேமா வடித்தற்றால்,
> நன்று அறியா மாந்தர்க்கு அறத்து ஆறு உரைக்குங்கால்;
> குன்றின்மேல் கொட்டும் தறிபோல் தலை தகர்ந்து
> சென்று இசையா ஆகும், செவிக்கு.

258. Charcoal will never go white even if you
　　　Wash it for days together with milk;
　　　As such for a man, destined not benevolently
　　　No knowledge would go in, even if you coerce him.

This poem raises a question whether men are congenitally wise or unwise. Is it right to link destiny with knowledge? It is up to the modern researchers to answer this question.

> பாலால் கழீஇ, பல நாள் உணக்கினும்,
> வாலிதாம் பக்கம் இருந்தைக்கு இருந்தன்று;
> கோலால் கடாஅய்க் குறினும், புகல் ஒல்லா,
> நோலா உடம்பிற்கு அறிவு.

259. Instead of flying towards fragrant flowers
　　　Fleas infatuate with dirty heaps of garbage;
　　　Likewise, what use the sweet and soft counsel
　　　Of great men would render to base-minded men?

To those who are fools and base – minded, no amount of counseling would do anything. Mere waste of time to advise the bad fellows of lower category.

> பொழிந்து இனிது நாறினும், பூ மிசைதல் செல்லாது,
> இழிந்தவை காமுறூஉம் ஈப்போல், இழிந்தவை
> தாம் கலந்த நெஞ்சினார்க்கு என் ஆகும், தக்கார் வாய்த்
> தேன் கலந்த தேற்றச் சொல் தேர்வு?

260. An ill bred vulgar wouldn't grasp immaculate
　　　And essential lessons of learned men and
　　　After a rejection of them by eyeing a similar
　　　Hollow man of his ilk, begin his own preaching to him.

One who is not able to genuinely grasp the intelligent counseling of great men, just to show that he is also equally capable, begin advising another hollow man of his own category.

கற்றார் உரைக்கும் கசடு அறு நுண் கேள்வி
பற்றாது தன் நெஞ்சு உதைத்தலால், மற்றும் ஓர்
தன்போல் ஒருவன் முகம் நோக்கி, தானும் ஓர்
புன்கோட்டி கொள்ளுமாம், கீழ்.

Chapter 27 - Useless Wealth
***

261. Bats wouldn't go to dry-barked *vilam* trees
    Even if there are nearer with a lot of fruits;
    Likewise, the wealth of undignified persons though near

    Is not amenable for the use of the poor.

Vilam is a gigantic tropical tree - Feronica elephantum. Its fruits are sweet but the shell is hard and hence no use for bats. They cannot break it. Similarly the wealth of the miserly persons would be of no use to the poor even when they are nearer to the needy.

> அருகுளது ஆகிப் பல பழுத்தக்கண்ணும்,
> பொரி தாள் விளவினை வாவல் குறுகா;-
> பெரிது அணியர் ஆயினும், பீடு இலார் செல்வம்
> கருதும் கடப்பாட்டது அன்று.

262. Even though buds are attractive, nobody
    Would touch the succulent plant as its flower is unfit
    To wear and likewise even if mean - minded are rich
    Men of knowledge and wiseness wouldn't go to them.

If wealth is abundant with loafers, it is of no use either to them or to the others who are in need of it. Such wealth is useless either to the rich or to the poor.

> அள்ளிக்கொள்வன்ன குறு முகிழ ஆயினும்,
> கள்ளிமேல் கைந் நீட்டார், சூடும் பூ அன்மையால்;-
> செல்வம் பெரிது உடையர் ஆயினும், கீழ்களை
> நள்ளார், அறிவுடையார்.

263. Though living on sea-shores, people go and drink
 Non-brackish well water of good spring and like-wise
 Even if non-generous rich are very near, men do not
 approach
 But go to willful donors, even if they are at a distance.

Men who live on coastal areas, very near the sea, cannot drink sea-water. Even at a distance, they go and drink well-water. Likewise even if miserly rich men are very near, people do not go to him but to a generous philanthropist they go even if he lives at a distance. What the poem implies is that the wealth that remains with miserly men is no of use to either of them.

> மல்கு திரைய கடற் கோட்டு இருப்பினும்,
> வல் ஊற்று உவர் இல் கிணற்றின்கண் சென்று உண்பர்;
> செல்வம் பெரிது உடையர் ஆயினும், சேண் சென்றும்
> நல்குவார்கட்டே நசை.

264. When wise men remain without resources
 Unwise like thorny bushes wear gorgeous apparel
 And lead a luxurious life; and on probing this
 Mysterious is the cause and effect of previous birth.

What men do in previous birth does not tally with their actions here in the present birth. That is why it is mysterious that unwise men are rich and wise men are poor. If so, the concept of pre-destinarian philosophy has become questionable,

> புணர் கடல் சூழ் வையத்துப் புண்ணியமோ வேறே
> உணர்வது உடையார் இருப்ப, உணர்வு இலா
> வட்டும் வழுதுணையும் போல்வாரும் வாழ்பவே,
> பட்டும் துகிலும் உடுத்து!

265. Ye, sharp-eyed damsel! When ethical and wise men
 Are indigent, the reason why the unwise and vicious
 Are richer is, nothing else but the fact of
 What they had done in their previous birth.

What has been expressed in the previous stanzas is pointed out as a mystery. If so does it mean that those who suffer poverty now have done bad things and those who are rich have done good things in the previous. If this is accepted, destiny has no place in a man's life.

> நல்லார் நயவர் இருப்ப, நயம் இலாக்
> கல்லார்க்கு ஒன்று ஆகிய காரணம், தொல்லை
> வினைப் பயன் அல்லது,-வேல் நெடுங் கண்ணாய்!
> நினைப்ப வருவது ஒன்று இல்.

266. Ye! The damsel, as dull as outer petal, sits over the
 Lotus flower! Leaving excellent good men behind
 You attach yourself with low bred vulgar and for
 Such uneven act, let you be consigned to flames.

No benefit to anybody if wealth goes to vicious and ill-bred people. In insisting on an appreciable idea, the poet doesn't mind cursing Lakshmi, the goddess of wealth.

> நாறாத் தகடே போல் நல் மலர்மேல் பொற்பாவாய்!
> நீறாய் நிலத்து விளிஅரோ-வேறு ஆய
> புன்மக்கள் பக்கம் புகுவாய் நீ, பொன் போலும்
> நன்மக்கள் பக்கம் துறந்து!

267. Ye, damsel of spear – like eyes! Has not indigence
 Felt shame to hold on honest men and is huge
                                                         wealth
 A glue to ever grow with men of no generosity?
 Be wondrous at this dislocation of poverty and
                                                         wealth.

Though the poem is addressed to a lady, what it implies is that rich men should be generous in financially helping others so that they could aim at an eternal pleasure. If honest men feel miserable for their poorness, it is a victory for poverty. Since they bear it with patience, poverty fails in its objective of harassing them. In spite of its failure, why should poverty hold them tightly? Has it not shame to do so, the poet asks.

> நயவார்கண் நல்குரவு நாண் இன்று கொல்லோ?
> பயவார்கண் செல்வம் பரம்பப் பயின்கொல்?
> வியவாய்காண்,-வேற் கண்ணாய்!-இவ் இரண்டும் ஆங்கே
> நயவாது நிற்கும் நிலை.

268. Shameful elders wander about and toil for
 Their mixed food in life but shameless beings
 Remain at home and eat roasted edible under
 The canopy with river water falling around from it.

Men of honesty earn for their livelihood by going around the places other than their own. But vicious elements of dishonesty somehow earn their wealth and enjoy eating mixed food of their own choice - under a built-in-canopy with holes on all sides of its ceiling with an arrangement of water falling down from it. A happy and comfortable life, they enjoy.

> வலவைகள் அல்லாதார், கால் ஆறு சென்று,
> கலவைகள் உண்டு, கழிப்பர்; வலவைகள்
> கால் ஆறும் செல்லார், கருணையால் துய்ப்பவே,
> மேல் ஆறு பாய, விருந்து.

269. When golden hued paddy crop with stalks
 Of young seeds yearn for water, cloudy rains
 Pour down on the sea and so also when men of
 Little sense get wealthy, their bounty is also similar.

Without quenching the thirst of paddy fields, clouds pour down their rains uselessly on the ocean. Similarly if unwise men become rich, they will be bounteous to undeserving people. Hence obviously the wealth of the senseless persons is spent uselessly.

பொன் நிறச் செந்நெல் பொதியொடு பீள் வாட,
மின் ஒளிர் வானம் கடலுள்ளும் கான்று உகுக்கும்-
வெண்மை உடையார் விழுச் செல்வம் எய்தியக்கால்,
வண்மையும் அன்ன தகைத்து.

270. Men of no wisdom, even if educated are uneducated;
With wisdom, even non-educated is like educated;
If doesn't beg, men of abject poverty are rich; if
Rich men are not generous, they are indigent.

Wealth brings honour, if only it is liberally spent on helping others. Wisdom brings a societal recognition and reputation, irrespective of whether the person is educated or not.

ஓதியும் ஓதார், உணர்வு இலார்; ஓதாதும்
ஓதி அனையார், உணர்வு உடையார்; தூய்து ஆக
நல்கூர்ந்தும் செல்வர், இரவாதார்; செல்வரும்
நல்கூர்ந்தார், ஈயார் எனின்.

Chapter 28 - Miserliness
***

Not extending financial help to those who seek charity or aid is miserliness. This is diametrically opposite to the virtuous quality of charity, grant or gift.

271. Happily sharing food moderately with those
 Who are related and friendly before eating oneself
 Is real house - keeping; but to those low-bred who
 Eat within closed doors, gates of paradise will be shut.

Generously sharing food with others is a gateway to Paradise. Saint Ramalingar in the South of India and Swami Bhakthi Vedanta of the USA's *Hare Krishna Movement* not only preached in favour of feeding others but practiced it also so long as they lived. Their disciples are bound to feed the power and the needy.

> நட்டார்க்கும் நள்ளாதவர்க்கும் உள வரையால்
> அட்டது பாத்து உண்டல், அட்டு உண்டல்; அட்டது
> அடைத்து இருந்து உண்டு ஒழுகும் ஆவது இல் மாக்கட்கு
> அடைக்குமாம், ஆண்டைக் கதவு.

272. Those who provide even little charity, to the extent
 Possible, would be deemed higher and the rest
 Who say, despite huge wealth that charity could be
 Done later, would be drowned in an ocean of sin.

Amount of charity, be big or small one extends is not a criteria but the mind of no miserliness in providing possible help to others is meant to be appreciated.

> எத்துணையானும், இயைந்த அளவினால்,
> சிற்றறம் செய்தார் தலைப்படுவர்; மற்றைப்
> பெருஞ் செல்வம் எய்தியக்கால், 'பின் அறிதும்!' என்பார்
> அழிந்தார், பழி கடலத்துள்.

273. Looking at a fool who neither enjoys himself
 Nor does he offer to the saints but expires will be
 Mocked at leaving riches behind, at length
 Wealth and also by the quality of mercy.

A man of miserliness will be humiliated and his wealth will of no use if it is not given to deserving poor.

துய்த்துக் கழியான், துறவோர்க்கு ஒன்று ஈகலான்,
வைத்துக் கழியும் மடவோனை,-வைத்த
பொருளும் அவனை நகுமே; உலகத்து
அருளும் அவனை நகும்.

274. Huge wealth of a miser who neither enjoys
 Himself nor does he grant to the needy will be
 Relished by others as does a family's ravishing
 Young damsels on maturity are enjoyed by some others.

Wealth that remains unspent will be taken over by others. Therefore one should be liberal in spending. That is the general theme of this unit. A comparison of dormant wealth with virgins is at odds on a deeper scrutiny. Virgins have necessarily to be married and hence they remain at home is natural. But a man's wealth should not be dormant and it has to be spent anyhow.

கொடுத்தலும், துய்த்தலும் தேற்றா இடுக்குடை
உள்ளத்தான் பெற்ற பெருஞ் செல்வம், இல்லத்து
உருவுடைக் கன்னியரைப் போல, பருவத்தால்,
ஏதிலான் துய்க்கப்படும்.

275. Though living adjacent to the sea of roaring waves
 Men go to drink water from a small well of little
     spring;
 Likewise, the indigence of great men is better than
     huge wealth of
 Misers who know not the benevolence of donation.

The poverty of great men who know the celestial benevolence of donations is better than the huge wealth of misers.

எறி நீர்ப் பெருங் கடல் எய்தி இருந்தும்,
அறு நீர்ச் சிறு கிணற்று ஊறல் பார்த்து உண்பர்;
மறுமை அறியாதார் ஆக்கத்தின், சான்றோர்
கழி நல்குரவே தலை.

276. The wealth of a foolish miser, I too would say
Mine; though it is owned by him, he doesn't
Give it to others nor does he enjoy it himself
And so also I too with that wealth.

The poet comments on the wealth of a foolish miser with sardonic amusement. So long as the wealth of a miser lies dormant, the poet says that he can also claim it as his own. If the miser spends it, he can establish it as his own. But he doesn't and hence the poet also logically claims that wealth as his own property.

'எனது எனது' என்று இருக்கும் ஏழை பொருளை,
'எனது எனது' என்று இருப்பன், யானும்; தனது ஆயின்,
தானும் அதனை வழங்கான்; பயன் துவ்வான்;
யானும் அதனை அது.

277. More than miserly rich, the penurious escaped from
The trouble of being pitied of having lost the wealth,
Safeguarding it, digging the ground to hide it
And of holding wealth in personal care among a few more.

Here also in a humorous way the poet says that a miserly fellow has got a lot of worries which a poor man doesn't have. He is relieved of being called a loser of money, bothered of safeguarding it and gotten rid of the burden of digging the ground to bury it. We are rest assured by the poet that there had been a habit of hiding solid wealth and valuables under the ground in olden days.

> வழங்காத செல்வரின், நல்கூர்ந்தார் உய்ந்தார்;
> இழந்தார் எனப்படுதல் உய்ந்தார்; உழந்து அதனைக்
> காப்பு உய்ந்தார்; கல்லுதலும் உய்ந்தார்; தம் கைந் நோவ
> யாப்பு உய்ந்தார்; உய்ந்த பல.

278. When the wealth is his, he won't donate;
Nor his heirs when it became theirs;
Had He denoted earlier, they wouldn't have objected
Nor he would if they have done it subsequently.

Degradation of abject miserliness is hinted at in this poem. The poet is at a loss why the original owner of wealth and also his descendants are equally bad and too stingy to give money to charitable causes. Typical useless of money is the substance of this stanza.

> தனது ஆகத் தான் கொடான்; தாயத்தவரும்
> தமது ஆய போழ்தே கொடாஅர்; தனது ஆக
> முன்னே கொடுப்பின், அவர் கடியார்; தான் கடியான்,
> பின்னை அவர் கொடுக்கும் போழ்து.

279. Charity it is to donate happily to beneficiaries
As a cow yields to its calf; downgraded charity it is
To donate after a strong persuasion as a cow that
Gives milk only when nipple of udders are pressed hard.

Desirable charity it is, if given with love and compassion; downgraded charity it is, if it is given on compulsion and coercion.

> இரவலர் கன்று ஆக, ஈவார் ஆ ஆக,
> விரகின் சுரப்பதாம், வண்மை; விரகு இன்றி
> வல்லவர் ஊன்ற வடி ஆபோல், வாய் வைத்துக்
> கொல்லச் சுரப்பதாம், கீழ்.

280. Earning is an ordeal and safeguarding
Such great wealth is misery, if its painful protection
Is lesser and if its damaged, a greater misery and
Thus wealth is an accumulated mass of agony.

What the poem implies is when such fallible and painful wealth is in our possession, it must be so spent on charitable ways that one would be able to have a peace of mind and happiness both in terrestrial world and celestial kingdom.

ஈட்டலும் துன்பம்; மற்று ஈட்டிய ஒண் பொருளைக்
காத்தலும் ஆங்கே கடுந் துன்பம்; காத்த
குறைபடின், துன்பம்; கெடின், துன்பம்; துன்பக்கு
உறைபதி, மற்றைப் பொருள்.

Chapter 29 – Poverty
***

Poverty is a situation of being poor and not having anything that is enjoyed by five senses of a human being. It is also known as indigence, impoverishment, penury, destitute and beggary. It has been said earlier that great men would ever be perturbed neither by penury nor by prosperity. But still, for any householder, material wealth is essential. If not, he will suffer in poverty. What type of travails he will undergo in his poverty - stricken life is enumerated here.

281. Even if lives with saffron cloth girdling the
     Waist, having money five or ten is honour to a man;
     Even if born in eminent family a man with
     No money will be deemed lower than a corpse.

Even if a man has renounced the pleasures of his worldly life and lead the life of a saint, if only he has money he will be respected. A man with no wealth, even if born in eminent family will be treated lower than a corpse.

அத்து இட்ட கூறை அரைச் சுற்றி வாழினும்,
பத்து எட்டு உடைமை பலருள்ளும் பாடு எய்தும்;
ஒத்த குடிப் பிறந்தக்கண்ணும், ஒன்று இல்லாதார்
செத்த பிணத்தின் கடை.

282. Ghee is said to be finer than water but everyone
     Knows smoke is thinner than ghee; if study deeper
     One who painfully begs will penetrate
     A hole through which even smoke cannot pass.

One who begs is the hardest hit financially. The pauper therefore does not mind any humiliation or insult but somehow penetrate a place where even smoke cannot go through. This is a hyperbolic statement.

> நீரினும் நுண்ணிது நெய் என்பர்; நெய்யினும்
> யாரும் அறிவர் புகை நுட்பம்; தேரின்,
> நிரப்பு இடும்பையாளன் புகுமே, புகையும்
> புகற்கு அரிய பூழை நுழைந்து.

283. Ye, Lord of hills where field guards catapult stones
To drive parrots out of corn fields! If red hibiscus
Does not blossom on the high, bees wouldn't go;
Likewise for penniless too, no relatives would go.

If a person is resourceful and rich, all and sundry will go to him to enjoy his benevolence. If he is pauper, nobody will go to him; nobody will like him rather. But poverty is the worst of all sufferings.

> கல் ஓங்கு உயர் வரைமேல் காந்தள் மலராக்கால்,
> செல்லாவாம், செம் பொறி வண்டுஇனம்;-கொல்லைக்
> கலாஅல் கிளி கடியும் கானக நாட!-
> இலாஅஅர்க்கு இல்லை, தமர்.

284. When a person is richer, thousands would gather
To serve him around as cluster of crows near a corpse;
But when he wanders about poorly like a fly
None to enquire him whether he is alright.

The implication is that no one would be concerned about persons who are penniless.

> உண்டாய போழ்தின், உடைந்துழிக் காகம்போல்,
> தொண்டு ஆயிரவர் தொகுபவே; வண்டாய்த்
> திரிதரும் காலத்து, 'தீது இலிரோ?' என்பார்
> ஒருவரும் இவ் உலகத்து இல்.

285. Ye Lord of hills where the roaring falls wash the
                                                boulders!
    To those who are stricken by poverty, eminence of
                                                their family
    Will go off; their pride of masculinity will
                                                disappear; even.
    Academic reputation of theirs will go
                                                unrecognized.

A man of poverty will not be recognized even if he had been born of a rich family; nor his knowledge ability also.

> பிறந்த குலம் மாயும்; பேர் ஆண்மை மாயும்;
> சிறந்த தம் கல்வியும் மாயும்;-கறங்கு அருவி
> கல்மேல் கழுஉம் கண மலை நல் நாட!-
> இன்மை தழுவப்பட்டார்க்கு.

286. One who is unable to quench the appetite
    Of those who have come within, despite being
    A local man, he can as well leave
    That place to be a guest elsewhere outside.

The meaning is that he need not reside there, even if he belongs to that place when he is unable to provide food for those suffer from hunger. He can as well go out of his place in search of food for him elsewhere. The poem implies that one should remain rich in his native place to help the poor and destitutes. If not he may go out of his native place in search of food and shelter.

> உள் கூர் பசியால் உழை நசைஇச் சென்றார்கட்கு,
> உள்ளூர் இருந்தும், ஒன்று ஆற்றாதான், உள்ளூர்
> இருந்து, உயிர் கொன்னே கழியாது, தான் போய்
> விருந்தினன் ஆதலே நன்று.

287. Ye Lady of so sharp and white teeth as to make even
 Mullai flower feel ashamed! Those who suffer
 from poverty
 Will be deprived of not only their virtues but also their
 Sharpness of intellect plus all its features as well.

Poverty stricken people will lose their good qualities such as virtues, intellect and shrewdness. Even their intelligence will not be recognised. That is the way of the world.

நீர்மையே அன்றி, நிரம்ப எழுந்த தம்
கூர்மையும் எல்லாம் ஒருங்கு இழப்பர்,-கூர்மையின்
முல்லை அலைக்கும் எயிற்றாய்!-நிரப்பு என்னும்
அல்லல் அடையப்பட்டார்.

288. One is unable to help those who beseech
 Due to poverty; instead of living in the same place
 With the same distress, journeying thro highway
 And indulge in beggary life in a row of homes is
 better.

Better to leave one's own place if unable to help others. Desirable to go elsewhere and begin begging there. Substance of this poem is the same as in stanza 286. But this cannot be blamed as a fault of repetitiveness because of the fact that each poem is said to be the contribution of each poet.

இட்டு ஆற்றுப்பட்டு, ஒன்று இரந்தவர்க்கு ஆற்றாது,
முட்டு ஆற்றுப்பட்டு, முயன்று, உள்ளூர் வாழ்தலின்,
நெட்டாற்றுச் சென்று, நிரை மனையில் கைந் நீட்டும்
கெட்ட ஆற்று வாழ்க்கையே நன்று.

289. When prosperity gets dried up, with those hands
 That once wore gold bracelets, they pluck
 Greens, boil them with no salt, eat them in poor
 Concave vessels and lead a life devoid of cheerfulness.

Even rich people suffer extremely if they have lost their wealth. Beggars receive alms in traditionally made wooden vessels, if they don't have metal pots. This is indicated in the poem as concave vessels.

> கடகம் செறிந்த தம் கைகளால் வாங்கி,
> அடகு பறித்துக்கொண்டு அட்டு, குடை கலனா,
> உப்பு இலி வெந்தை தின்று, உள் அற்று, வாழ்பவே
> துப்புரவு சென்று உலந்தக்கால்.

290. Ye, Lord of cool hillocks of perennial cascades!
    Beautifully spotted swarm of bees will never
    Fly to tree branches that have flowers no longer;
    Likewise, no relatives to those who are destitutes.

That means no relative would go anywhere near a person who is suffering from poverty. Rich and resourceful person alone will be respected. Even relatives would never recognise and respect them. Poverty is such deplorable existence.

> ஆர்த்த பொறிய அணி கிளர் வண்டுஇனம்
> பூத்து ஒழி கொம்பின்மேல் செல்லாவாம்;-நீர்த்து அருவி
> தாழா உயர் சிறப்பின் தண் குன்ற நல் நாட!
> வாழாதார்க்கு இல்லை, தமர்.

Chapter 30 - Self Respect
***

The dignity of safeguarding self-respect and the disgrace in losing it are explained in this chapter. What annuls the self-respect are poverty and beggary. If these two things are kept at a distance, one can easily maintain his self-respect.

291. Wealth, as their strength a few vicious mean-minded
 Behave exceedingly bad and on seeing this,
 Men of self-respect will burn within
 As furiously as a huge forest - fire.

Men of self – respect will be extremely annoyed when the low-bred wealthy men act unwisely. Their mind will burn within as much as a raging wild fire.

> திரு மதுகையாகத் திறன் இலார் செய்யும்
> பெருமிதம் கண்டக்கடைத்தும், எரி மண்டிக்
> கானம் தலைப்பட்ட தீப்போல் கனலுமே
> மானம் உடையார் மனம்.

292. When dignified men become bonny and suffer
 Will they go behind unwise to narrate their misery?
 Will they not narrate their distress to wise men
 Who could be prescient of it earlier than they say it?

Without revealing their suffering to ill – natured persons, men of self-respect will make a report only to those wise men who could even be aware of their misery much earlier than they say it.

> என்பாய் உகினும், இயல்பு இலார் பின் சென்று,
> தம் பாடு உரைப்பரோ, தம் உடையார்? தம் பாடு
> உரையாமை முன் உணரும் ஒண்மை உடையார்க்கு
> உரையாரோ, தாம் உற்ற நோய்?

293. We would, to visitors show our home but arrogant
 Wealthy men do not, as if its beauty get spoiled;
 So, they treat us by feeding us in the backyard;
 Forget for ever such wealthy people.

The poem is purported to have been reported by a poverty - stricken man to his friend. The idea behind the poem is that men of self – respect should give up the friendship of such arrogant and wealthy persons.

யாம் ஆயின் எம் இல்லம் காட்டுதும்; தாம் ஆயின்,
காணவே கற்பு அழியும் என்பார்போல், நாணி,
புறங்கடை வைத்து ஈவர், சோறும்; அதனால்
மறந்திடுக, செல்வர் தொடர்பு!

294. Ye, the lady of musk flavoured locks of hair!
 Dignified quality of self-respected - men is a
 Matter of reputation in the present birth; also
 Creditable in the other birth and hence it's benevolent.

Those who are interested in securing pleasure in life, both terrestrial and celestial must maintain their self-dignity.

இம்மையும் நன்று ஆம்; இயல் நெறியும் கைவிடாது,
உம்மையும் நல்ல பயத்தலால்,-செம்மையின்
நானம் கமழும் கதுப்பினாய்!-நன்றேகாண்,
மானம் உடையார் மதிப்பு.

295. Great men wouldn't do any act of sin
 And shame even at the risk of death
 Which is a matter of distress for a day
 And do not do the unbearable misery as the other two.

Death causes painful misery for a day; but sin and shame for days on end give unbearable agony. Hence great men would not commit them on any ground whatsoever, even if death comes to them.

> பாவமும் ஏனைப் பழியும் பட வருவ,
> சாயினும், சான்றவர் செய்கலார்;-சாதல்
> ஒருநாள் ஒரு பொழுதைத் துன்பம்; அவைபோல்
> அரு நவை ஆற்றுதல் இன்று.

296. Of all who live in the prosperous fertile world
Those who don't help destitute are virtual poor
Even though rich; those who don't beseech that rich
In their poverty are like as rich as Mutharaiyar.

Mutharaiyar ought to have been a very rich man at a time when the poet was composing this stanza. It is also the title of a royal clan that ruled a part of Chola territory with Senthalai as its capital.

> மல்லல் மா ஞாலத்து வாழ்பவருள் எல்லாம்
> செல்வர் எனினும், கொடாதவர் நல்கூர்ந்தார்;
> நல்கூர்ந்தக்கண்ணும், பெரு முத்தரையரே,
> செல்வரைச் சென்று இரவாதார்.

297. Ye, the spear – like brow and wide – eyed lady! Lower
Men would be worried of their painful hunger;
Mediocres for their impending distress but
The higher men would be afraid of the reproach of
others.

Those who safeguard the self-respect on any account in spite of worldly difficulties are categorized as the first; the mediocre are afraid of the unpleasant experiences in life and hence they are number two. Those of the last category are plainly practical and worried of their day to day needs. Hence they are of the lowest level.

கடை எலாம் காய் பசி அஞ்சும்; மற்று ஏனை
இடை எலாம் இன்னாமை அஞ்சும்;-புடை உலாம்
விற் புருவ வேல் நெடுங் கண்ணாய்!-தலை எலாம்
சொற் பழி அஞ்சிவிடும்.

298. When wily rich dart a condemning look saying
This is a great man, merciful but became very poor,
May be the mind of the great would burn within
As the smouldering fire of a furnace in a smithy.

Great men would feel miserably embittered, if they are ludicrously great men commented upon by the rich men of cunningness. Feeling of those great would burned within, on such occasions.

'நல்லர்! பெரிது அளியர்! நல்கூர்ந்தார்!' என்று எள்ளி,
செல்வர் சிறு நோக்கு நோக்குங்கால், கொல்லன்
உலை ஊதும் தீயேபோல் உள் கனலும் கொல்லோ,
தலையாய சான்றோர் மனம்.

299. Not a shame if nothing is given to those who
Expected from us; shameful due to fear is also
Not a disgrace; but shame it is, in disclosing
Ignominy cast on our poverty by arrogant rich.

The best in life is to safeguard our dignity. Having been insulted by a rich man is ignominy. Sensitive persons will feel ashamed even to think of it. That is the most shameful thing to be avoided.

நச்சியார்க்கு ஈயாமை நாண் அன்று; நாள் நாளும்,
அச்சத்தால் நாணுதல் நாண் அன்றாம்; எச்சத்தின்
மெல்லியர் ஆகித் தம் மேலாயார் செய்தது
சொல்லாது இருப்பது-நாண்.

300. If a wild cow attacked by a jungle - tiger
Falls on left, it wouldn't eat it; likewise
Even if the heavenly world is to come at the
Expense of dignity, great men would never opt for it.

Men of self-respect would not consider anything as great other than dignity. Self dignity alone they will respect. Example drawn from the supposed habit of a tiger is subject to the confirmation of tiger-hunters.

கடமா தொலைச்சிய கான் உறை வேங்கை
இடம் வீழ்ந்தது உண்ணாது இறக்கும்;-இடமுடைய
வானகம் கையுறினும் வேண்டார், விழுமியோர்,
மானம் அழுங்க வரின்.

Chapter – 31. Fear of beggary
***

Begging is a disgrace. Men of dignity will earn for their livelihood and never think of begging. In fact they will be afraid of leading such a dishonourable life. It is about their fear and hesitation towards begging, this chapter speaks.

301. Will any knowledgeable person follow those
 Who are self-conceited and of egoistic mind – set
 Who think these indigent men get rich due to myself;
 They have nothing out of their own efforts".

Persons who think that 'others are inert and do not earn by themselves; whatever they have, is because of my efforts.' are self-conceited. No sensitive person will be un happy to avoid him. He would never approach such egoistic persons to get help.

'நம்மாலே ஆவர், இந் நல்கூர்ந்தார்; எஞ் ஞான்றும்
தம்மால் ஆம் ஆக்கம் இலர்' என்று, தம்மை
மருண்ட மனத்தார்பின் செல்பவோ, தாழும்
தெருண்ட அறிவினவர்?

302. Is it wrong to be in fast and hunger instead of eating
 A lot, after doing degraded actions?
 Doesn't the rebirth of a man occur in so
 Short a time as much as that of winking of an eye?

Because, rebirth occurs so soon, as much of a time as taken for winking of eye lids. Such being the case, even if a man dies out of hunger, there is nothing wrong. He is bound to be born soon. What is important therefore is that one should not degrade himself by begging to quench his appetite. Better to die rather than begging.

இழித்தக்க செய்து ஒருவன் ஆர உணலின்,
பழித்தக்க செய்யான், பசித்தல் தவறோ?-
விழித்து இமைக்கும் மாத்திரை அன்றோ, ஒருவன்
அழித்துப் பிறக்கும் பிறப்பு.

303. Driven by abject poverty a few cannot but
Boldly implore others; but will they wilfully
Go and see the others' face excepting to those great
Who would embrace saying, "Get in, eat with us inside"

Men in poverty at times cannot but go and beg others. When they do so, they choose only those who would generously welcome them and offer food but they wouldn't go to others, unless driven by abject poverty and distress.

இல்லாமை கந்தா இரவு துணிந்து, ஒருவர்
செல்லாரும் அல்லர், சிறு நெறி; புல்லா,
'அகம் புகுமின்; உண்ணுமின்' என்பவர்மாட்டு அல்லால்,
முகம்புகுதல் ஆற்றுமோ, மேல்?

304. Even if rejected by Goddess of wealth or
If angered by God, highly dignified man
Instead of pursuing further, would not go
With a bowed head before the foolish misers.

They would continue to strive hard to earn of their own accord. What the poem counsels is that if poor but dignified people are in distress or poverty, they should not go to wealthy misers but pursue their own efforts to earn wealth.

திருத் தன்னை நீப்பினும், தெய்வம் செறினும்,
உருத்த மனத்தோடு உயர்வு உள்ளின் அல்லால்,
அருத்தம் செறிக்கும் அறிவிலார் பின் சென்று,
எருத்து இறைஞ்சி நில்லாதாம், மேல்.

305. The best is one who does no begging even from
 Those highly endearing men, capable of gifting
 Liberally; when our mind weeps at thinking beggary
 What else be the mind of men at the time of their
 begging?

Begging in any way is unpleasant, pitiable and miserable, besides being low and degraded. This is emphatically asserted in this stanza.

> கரவாத திண் அன்பின் கண் அன்னார்கண்ணும்
> இரவாது வாழ்வது ஆம் வாழ்க்கை; இரவினை
> உள்ளுங்கால் உள்ளம் உருகுமால்; என்கொலோ,
> கொள்ளுங்கால் கொள்வார் குறிப்பு?

306. Poverty wouldn't hurt if one is in balanced
 Mind of not deeming delight and distress as such
 And so why should he beg others passionately
 With sight - failing sunken eyes?

He would never degrade himself by begging others. Such a man of spiritual intellect will be dispassionate for delight as well as distress. Both the qualities are equal to him. Such a man of balanced mind need not disgrace himself into begging. This is what the poem enunciates.

> 'இன்னா இயைக, இனிய ஒழிக' என்று
> தன்னையே தான் இரப்பத் தீர்வதற்கு, என்னைகொல்,
> காதல் கவற்றும் மனத்தினால் கண் பாழ்பட்டு
> ஏதிலவரை இரவு?

307. Ye, Lord of a land where cascades raging widely
 And scatter golden-hued sand! Even though
 New born ever in the world, an excellent man is
 The one who never humiliates the mendicants:

The idea behind the poem is that those who die are supposed to be born again and again in this world; but those who never insult and humiliate the beggars will never undergo a rebirth. They are due to attain *'moksha'* or celestial habitation. There had been a belief in re-birth. But great men desire that they should not be born again.

என்றும் புதியார் பிறப்பினும், இவ் உலகத்து,
என்றும் அவனே பிறக்கலான்-குன்றின்
பரப்பு எலாம் பொன் ஒழுகும் பாய் அருவி நாட!
இரப்பாரை எள்ளா மகன்.

308. With poverty afflicts worldly life, setting
Aside shame from his mind and pleaded
For alms from a man but still if that person
Returned emptily, would he not die forthwith?

Giving up shame, one man goes for alms. If he is returned with nothing from the donor, that man who implored may even die out of mental agony.

புறத்துத் தன் இன்மை நலிய, அகத்துத் தன்
நல் ஞானம் நீக்கி நிறீஇ, ஒருவனை,
'ஈயாய் எனக்கு!' என்று இரப்பானேல், அந் நிலையே
மாயானோ, மாற்றிவிடின்?

309. Disciplined it is for one to move friendly with
Another, but is the poverty which he now undergoes
Is more painful than using shameless phrases of
                                                                      Beggary,
"Would he not give me anything?"

In case of doing work as a subordinate and get help when suffering from poverty is alright. But on that score, he should not shamelessly ask anything merely as a charity. That kind of beggary is a great disgrace.

ஒருவர் ஒருவரைச் சார்ந்து ஒழுகல் ஆற்றி,
வழிபடுதல் வல்லுதல் அல்லால், பரிசு அழிந்து,
'செய்யீரோ, என்னானும்!' என்னும் சொற்கு இன்னாதே,
பையத் தாம் செல்லும் நெறி?

310. If one approaches another on the basis of
By-gone friendship, he must give the man
Some help but if he doesn't, the one who sought help
Will keep it in mind which will be like blazing fire.

Imploration is a shameful act. But if anybody on the basis of intimacy of olden days comes, the host should extend some amount of help. Otherwise, the man who came imploring will suffer within.

பழமை கந்தாகப் பசைந்த வழியே
கிழமைதான் யாதானும் செய்க! கிழமை
பொறாஅர் அவர் என்னின், பொத்தி, தம் நெஞ்சத்து
அறாஅச் சுடுவது ஓர் தீ.

Chapter – 32 Aware of Audience
***

This is the quality of being aware of the audience in a hall or a chamber. This awareness will be enlightening to behave suitably in the assembly of intellectuals. Otherwise, any person may behave erratically and will be subjected to dishonor and shame.

311. In the presence of murky thinkers who gave up
     Scholastic traits but exposed their ignorance
     Reiterated the same and behave badly,
     Men of genius will never reveal their expertise.

Intellectual personages have to be silent before certain idiotic elements who, time and again expose their little knowledge in the assemblage of geniuses instead of deferentially increasing their learning there. *A little knowledge is a dangerous thing,* says Alexander Pope, an 18" cent English poet.

> மெய்ஞ் ஞானக் கோட்டி உறழ்வழி விட்டு, ஆங்கு ஓர்
> அஞ்ஞானம் தந்திட்டு, அது ஆங்கு அறத் துழாய்,
> கைஞ் ஞானம் கொண்டு ஒழுகும் காரறிவாளர் முன்,
> சொல் ஞானம் சோர விடல்!

312. Scholarly great wouldn't join with ignoble lettered
     Men who gather a crowd of listeners for their blabbering
     Expositions; because such a man may even hurl
     A communal insult or initiate a physical combat.

Genuine scholars of erudition have to keep at a distance those who are masquerading as great learners and blabber incoherently with a set of their yes-men and henchmen.

> நாப் பாடம் சொல்லி நயம் உணர்வார்போல் செறிக்கும்
> தீப் புலவற் சேரார், செறிவுடையார்; தீப் புலவன்
> கோட்டியுள், குன்றக் குடி பழிக்கும்; அல்லாக்கால்,
> தோள் புடைக்கொள்ளா எழும்.

313. Persons are there enamoured of hot verbal arguing
Unrealising their limited learning and eloquence,
Unaware of effectively elucidate what little they learnt
Plus their failure but indulge in mere verbosity.

Such men of hollowness are of no use to any assembly of learned intellectuals. Better for them in not mingling with an intellectual group.

> சொல்-தாற்றுக் கொண்டு சுனைத்து எழுதல் காமுறுவர்,
> கற்ற ஆற்றல் வன்மையும் தாம் தேறார், கற்ற
> செல உரைக்கும் ஆறு அறியார், தோற்பது அறியார்,
> பல உரைக்கும் மாந்தர் பலர்.

314. Devoid of learning anything in full but
Having heard the content of one sutra from a teacher
A fool exposes himself unashamedly amidst
Veteran scholars and betray his little knowledge.

One should be aware of the scholarly audience and behave accordingly instead of foolishly betraying his idiocy.

> கற்றதூஉம் இன்றி, கணக்காயர் பாடத்தால்
> பெற்றதாம் பேதை ஓர் சூத்திரம்; மற்று அதனை
> நல்லாரிடைப் புக்கு, நாணாது சொல்லி, தன்
> புல்லறிவு காட்டிவிடும்.

315. Those who wisely argue for winning in debate
Along with those who behave beastly without seeing
Truth but stand up furiously and use harsh words
Will see into hands their teeth as white as gourd seeds.

Persons brutally behave in argument, using harsh words will render a punishment of breaking the teeth of sane - minded great men who attempt counselling to them; so, it is better to know the quality and behavioural pattern of who come to argue with us.

> வென்றிப் பொருட்டால் விலங்கு ஒத்து, மெய் கொள்ளார்,
> கன்றிக் கறுத்து எழுந்து, காய்வாரோடு ஒன்றி,
> உரை வித்தகம் எழுவார் காண்பவே, கையுள்
> சுரை வித்துப் போலும் தம் பல்.

316. When ignorant fool speaks condemnable
 Things, harmless good men felt sympathetic
 For the mother who had begotten
 That fool and tolerate his nonsense.

If scholarly men expose the ignorance of the fool, it will be a shame to him. May be his mother too will be ashamed. To prevent such eventuality, great men will bear with the idiocy of fools but feel pity for the mother for having begotten such a foolish person.

> பாடமே ஓதிப் பயன் தெரிதல் தேற்றாத
> மூடர் முனிதக்க சொல்லுங்கால், கேடு அருஞ்சீர்ச்
> சான்றோர் சமழ்த்தனர் நிற்பவே, மற்று அவரை
> ஈன்றாட்கு இறப்பப் பரிந்து.

317. To all those who begin formal learning, books
 Will be easily comprehensive as the shoulders of
                                                                whores;
 But the finer content of books will be rare to grasp
 As the mind of those soft bodied ladies.

Cursory learning is as easier as that of getting the company of a prostitute. But grasping the content of any book will be very difficult as much as that of studying her mind. Needless to say that whoever gives more, a whore will go behind such a person. What the poem attempts to say is that an assembly of those who grasp the ins and outs of any treatise is worthy of appreciation.

பெறுவது கொள்பவர் தோள்போல், நெறிபட்டுக்
கற்பவர்க்கு எல்லாம் எளிய, நூல்; மற்று அம்
முறி புரை மேனியர் உள்ளம் போன்று, யார்க்கும்
அறிதற்கு அரிய, பொருள்.

318. There are many who merely collect and gather
The books all over the house, not knowing
What they contain; those who safeguard them is
One group; learn and make others learn is another.

Counterfeit scholars are those who simply collect books and make it showy for others. Real scholars are those who not merely gather books, but read them continuously and constantly besides making others also understand them. An assembly of such deep scholars is fit for a constant association and contact.

புத்தகமே சாலத் தொகுத்தும், பொருள் தெரியார்,
உய்த்து, அகம் எல்லாம் நிறைப்பினும், மற்று அவற்றைப்
போற்றும் புலவரும் வேறே; பொருள் தெரிந்து
தேற்றும் புலவரும் வேறு.

319. Ye, Lord who owns so fertile a hill that draws
A herd of wild cows around it! Will the commentary
Of a scholar be the best, if not inclusive of paraphrase,
Explanatory notes, thematic points and an abstract.

In editing a poetical version of a book, either an anthology or a single work, it should contain all the four types of explanation. This point is valid only for books of the by-gone ages. In modern days, authors believe in simple language whether it is prose or poetry. Hence, a need for such an elaborate and descriptive explanation has not arisen for most of the modern lifeway outputs.

பொழிப்பு, அகலம், நுட்பம், நூல் எச்சம், இந் நான்கின்
கொழித்து, அகலம் காட்டாதார் சொற்கள், பழிப்பு இல்
நிரை ஆமா சேக்கும் நெடுங் குன்ற நாட!
உரை ஆமோ, நூலிற்கு நன்கு?

320. Will those born of ignoble families, however learned
 Ever be humble without speaking ill of others?
 But great scholars never take cognizance of
 Such poor knowledge of those men in ancient
 works.

Those born of dignified families never speak disparagingly of other's poor knowledge. They will overlook it. There lies their majestic outlook. But those of ignoble families will find fault and speak ill of the little knowledge of others.

இற் பிறப்பு இல்லார் எனைத்து நூல் கற்பினும்,
சொல் பிறரைக் காக்கும் கருவியரோ? இற் பிறந்த
நல் அறிவாளர், நவின்ற நூல் தேற்றாதார்
புல்லறிவு தாம் அறிவது இல்.

Chapter 33 – Ignorance
***

Intellectuals are those who are known for their deep knowledge and understanding. They are of high calibre in revealing their competence and talent. Just opposite to these qualities are of those who consider themselves as so great without realising their hollowness. It is about these hollow men, this chapter speaks.

321. Learned will find it useful whatever that is
     Preached by great intellects of love and grace;
     Not so the man of poor in eloquence as
     A wooden ladle doesn't know the sweetness of
     milky gruel.

Men who lack intellectual capacity will not respect and value the learned counselling of great men. Those of such disrespectful quality are like a big spoon or ladle that doesn't know the delicious nutritional value of porridge or gruel.

அருளின் அறம் உரைக்கும் அன்புடையார் வாய்ச் சொல்
பொருள் ஆகக் கொள்வர், புலவர்; பொருள் அல்லா
ஏழை அதனை இகழ்ந்து உரைக்கும், பாற்கூழை
மூழை சுவை உணராதாங்கு.

322. When virtues are preached by great men
     Men of poor intellect will pay no heed of them;
     As a pulaiyars dog that enjoys munching of dry hide
     Wouldn't relish a food cooked with milk.

Pulaiyas are men who bury the carcass of dead animals. Dogs that are brought up by them may not be accustomed to eat rich milky food. Those persons who don't understand the ethical value of virtues preached by learned men are therefore compared to the dogs of pulaiyas.

அவ்வியம் இல்லார் அறத்து ஆறு உரைக்குங்கால்,
செவ்வியர் அல்லார் செவி கொடுத்தும் கேட்கலார்-
கவ்வித் தோல் தின்னும் குணுங்கர் நாய் பாற்சோற்றின்
செவ்வி கொளல் தேற்றாதாங்கு.

323. Even though aware that our temporal life
 May cease to be in a wink of time,
 There are men who don't do even iota of charity
 What is it whether they are alive or dead.

No one can predict the day of death. It may occur at any moment. In such an uncertainty, what the poem counsels is to extend any help that you can to those who are in straitened circumstances.

இமைக்கும் அளவில் தம் இன் உயிர் போம் ஆற்றை
எனைத்தானும் தாம் கண்டு இருந்தும், திணைத் துணையும்
நன்றி புரிகல்லா, நாண் இல் மட மாக்கள்
பொன்றில் என்? பொன்றாக்கால் என்?

324. Span of life limited, safeguard is nil
 But yet, calumny in life is countless;
 Hence what use is it to isolate oneself
 Without happily mingling with others.

Nature of human life is transitory. Longevity of life is not assured. In such a short-lived nature of life, there are many who find fault with us. In such a problematic existence, why should a man morosely isolate himself without freely and happily mingling with fellow beings?.

உளநாள் சிலவால்; உயிர்க்கு ஏமம் இன்றால்;
பலர் மன்னும் தூற்றும் பழியால்; பலருள்ளும்
கண்டாரோடு எல்லாம் நகாஅது, எவன் ஒருவன்,
தண்டி, தனிப்பகை கோள்?

325. One has insulted and his talent in a forum
 Still if the blamed hasn't retorted to it
 In the same vein, wonder it is
 If the accuser retains happy in life.

One has blamed another person publicly in front of others. But yet, the insulted has not reacted harshly but maintained a good composure. If so, the accuser cannot be happy. His conscience will prick him for having insulted a good man. It will be surprising if he is happy in life. The poet implies that a sense of toleration is worthy of emulation.

எய்தி இருந்த அவைமுன்னர்ச் சென்று, எள்ளி,
வைதான், ஒருவன் ஒருவனை; வைய,
வயப்பட்டான் வாளா இருப்பானேல், வைதான்
வியத்தக்கான், வாழும் எனின்.

326. If not awaken sense of charity and spur it on
 Earlier than the advent of agedness in life,
 One would be subjected even in his home
 To be neglected, ordered to be out, even by a maid.

Extending benevolent actions, earlier than becoming old and decrepit are emphasised here. If not a situation of being reflected by even a servant maid may happen at an old age, warns the poet.

மூப்பு மேல் வாராமை முன்னே, அறவினையை
ஊக்கி, அதன்கண் முயலாதான், நூக்கி,
'புறத்து இரு; போகு' என்னும் இன்னாச் சொல் இல்லுள்
தொழுத்தையால் கூறப்படும்.

327. Neither will they enjoy nor do good for the great
 Nor be attached to benevolent way of life but
 Infatuated with materialistic way of life
 The poor intellect will spend their days in vain.

Persons with lesser eloquence will never enjoy their life nor will they render help to the deserving poor. Without realising that materialistic way of life is inconstant, they spend their life uselessly.

> தாமேயும் இன்புறார்; தக்கார்க்கும் நன்று ஆற்றார்;
> ஏமம் சார் நல் நெறியும் சேர்கலார்; தாம் மயங்கி
> ஆக்கத்துள் தூங்கி, அவத்தமே வாழ்நாளைப்
> போக்குவார்-புல்லறிவினார்.

328. Those who don't themselves do charitable
　　　But go on postponed it are of lesser knowledge-
　　　At the fag end of life, when they gesture for
　　　Their saving of solid gold, wood-apple may come.

If a person belatedly think of doing good to others and demand his saving of gold by a gesture, his wife or next of him may bring wood-apple fruit. What he ought to have done is that he must have helped others when he was young.

> சிறுகாலையே தமக்குச் செல்வுழி வல்சி
> இறுகிறுகத் தோட்கோப்புக் கொள்ளார், இறுகிறுகி,
> 'பின் அறிவாம்' என்று இருக்கும் பேதையார், கை காட்டும்
> பொன்னும் புளி விளங்காய் ஆம்.

329. Persons of poor intellect think of doing good
　　　In a changed mind in their illness and poverty;
　　　Not even an iota of charity they did think
　　　When they were rich and enjoyed a healthy life.

One should do benevolent actions and extent help to others only at a time when he was young, healthy and rich. No use in thinking of good deeds when he himself has fallen ill and poor. It is about these poor men of knowledge, the poem feels pity.

> வெறுமை இடத்தும், விழுப் பிணிப் போழ்தும்,
> மறுமை மனத்தாரே ஆகி, மறுமையை
> ஐந்தை அனைத்தானும், ஆற்றிய காலத்துச்
> சிந்தியார் சிற்றறிவினார்.

330. Despite having human life, never think of
 Charitable deeds but spend their life vainly;
 That too after seeing the endearing lives of
 Kith and kin are snatched away by yama.

Human life is the precious gift of God. It is a chance given to do charitable acts. But in no time that human life is snatched away by yama, the god of death. Fully realising that the duration of earthly life is short and unsure it is a pity that men of poor intellect do not perform charitable acts.

என்னே!-மற்று இவ் உடம்பு பெற்றும் அறம் நினையார்,
கொன்னே கழிப்பர் தம் வாழ்நாளை, அன்னோ!
அளவு இறந்த காதல் தம் ஆர் உயிர் அன்னார்க்
கொள இழைக்கும் கூற்றமும் கண்டு.

Chapter 34 – Idiocy
***

Not knowing anything is total ignorance. Allied to delusion. A bit of knowledge is also not desirable. Alexander Pope, an 18th century English poet has said, *"Little Knowledge is a dangerous Thing"*. This chapter elucidates definition of 'ignorance and enumerates its consequences in worldly life.

331. Unaware of murderous intent of God of death
     To snatch human life, the role of men who are ecstatic
     In a trap of worldly life is like a turtle
     Playfully swims in water set on fire by its killers.

Foolish men are under a delusion that this worldly life is permanent, not realizing that it is likely to be snatched away by God of Death at any time. Their ignorance is equal to that of a tortoise that swims in water - pot set on fire by its killer.

> கொலைஞர் உலை ஏற்றித் தீ மடுப்ப, ஆமை
> நிலை அறியாது அந் நீர் படிந்தாடியற்றே
> கொலை வல் கொடுங் கூற்றம் கோள் பார்ப்ப, ஈண்டை
> வலையகத்துச் செம்மாப்பார் மாண்பு.

332. Quality of a person who merely plans to do charities
     After fulfilling all domestic obligations
     Is like that of a man gone to have a dip in the sea,
                                                    decided
     To wait until the roaring of waves is over.

What the poem implies is that one should do whatever charities that are possible to him in no time, without waiting for an opportune moment. Waiting for an occasion to do benevolent activities is like waiting for a calm sea to take bath.

பெருங் கடல் ஆடிய சென்றார், 'ஒருங்கு உடன்
ஓசை அவிந்தபின் ஆடுதும்' என்றற்றால்-
'இல் செய் குறைவினை நீக்கி, அறவினை
மற்று அறிவாம்' என்று இருப்பார் மாண்பு.

333. Though a person has achieved the heritage
Of birth, penance, education, family growth
And maturity, he being unaware of faultless
Celestial sense is like boiled rice with no ghee.

Importance of celestial knowledge is emphasized in this stanza. Even though a person is competent in education and maturity in knowledge, it is of no use if he doesn't know the merits of celestial path.

குலம், தவம், கல்வி, குடிமை, மூப்பு ஐந்தும்
விலங்காமல் எய்தியக்கண்ணும், நலம் சான்ற
மை அறு தொல் சீர் உலகம் அறியாமை
நெய் இலாப் பாற்சோற்றின் நேர்.

334. Though not comprehend man's speech,
Boulders oblige persons to stand, sit, lie down and
Walk on them and so, they are far superior
To the low - level men of no help to anybody.

A strange idea that is expressed here is that solid rocky stones are better than low - bred men who does no help to anybody. This is in a way comparable to *Tirukkural* -151- which says that one should bear with those who insult us as the land-mass tolerate those who dig and cut it.

"To bear with those who revile us, even as the earth
bears up those who dig it, is the first of virtues" - W.H. Drew.

கல் நனி நல்ல, கடை ஆய மாக்களின்-
சொல் நனி தாம் உணரா ஆயினும், இன்னினியே
நிற்றல், இருத்தல், கிடத்தல், இயங்குதல், என்று
உற்றவர்க்குத் தாம் உதவலான்.

335. No use for him to do so but as if he has got it
He angrily scold the undeserving men with
Abusive words; unless he does it, the ill – bred
Man's tongue would continue to itch him to do the
mischief.

A mischievous fellow's vicious psyche of finding fault with and speaking ill of good people for reasons known to none, is exemplified in this stanza.

> பெறுவது ஒன்று இன்றியும், பெற்றானே போலக்
> கறுவுகொண்டு, ஏலாதார்மாட்டும், கறுவினால்
> கோத்து இன்னா கூறி உரையாக்கால், பேதைக்கு
> நாத் தின்னும், நல்ல சுனைத்து!

336. Ye Lord of the coast where flourishes rich leafy
Punnai!
A few say they would get along with vicious idiots
And make them amenable; such a puny effort
Is like losing the nail in pinching the rock.

Idiotic fellows cannot be amended. Even if anybody take efforts to make them alright, their efforts will prove to be unsuccessful.

> தம்கண் அமர்பு இல்லார்பின் சென்று, தாம், 'அவரை
> எம்கண் வணக்குதும் ' என்பவர் புன் கேண்மை
> நல் தளிர்ப் புன்னை மலரும் கடற் சேர்ப்ப!
> கல் கிள்ளிக் கை இழந்தற்று.

337. Though ants can't browse the ghee in a closed
Container, they would swarm around it and likewise
Even though rich men do not give anything to needy,
Indigent men would not go away from them.

Men of ignorance credulously go around rich men hoping that they would be favoured. But the fact that it is a false hope has been explained in this stanza.

ஆகாதுஎனினும், அகத்து நெய் உண்டாகின்,
போகாது எறும்பு புறம் சுற்றும்;-யாதும்
கொடாஅர் எனினும், உடையாரைப் பற்றி
விடாஅர், உலகத்தவர்.

338. Stupid men do no good daily; nor charity; don't
Give benefaction to poor; nor embrace the shoulders
Of a deserving wife; nor do they live famously;
What else can they do except hating their life?

Life will be useless for such stupid persons when they don't do any one of the benevolent activities listed out in the stanza. The world will derive no benefit from them. Theirs is an ignorance and idiocy.

நல்லவை நாள்தொறும் எய்தார்; அறம் செய்யார்;
இல்லாதார்க்கு யாது ஒன்றும் ஈகலார்; எல்லாம்
இனியார் தோள் சேரார்; இசைபட வாழார்;-
முனியார்கொல் தாம் வாழும் நாள்?

339. A Self-centred arrogant man doesn't have a
Sense of respect even to those who honour him;
Intimacy with such prideful man is unpalatable
Even if the world girded by a sea of roaring waves
                              is offered.

Friendship with those arrogant persons who don't respect even those who are desirable. Attempting to befriend them is absolutely idiotic. One should not be too ignorant to initiate camaraderie.

விழைந்து ஒருவர் தம்மை வியப்ப, ஒருவர்
விழைந்திலேம் என்று இருக்கும் கேண்மை, தழங்குரல்
பாய் திரை சூழ் வையம் பயப்பினும், இன்னாதே-
ஆய் நலம் இல்லாதார்மாட்டு.

340. One would get honour, if others speak well
 Of his scholarship, wide reputation, and noble birth;
 If he himself boasts of them, he would be scorned
 As an incurable lunatic by a large number of those
 who mock at him.

Real merit and efficiency should be respected by others without soliciting for it. If shamelessly boasts of himself, he will be ridiculed by the world outside.

கற்றனவும், கண் அகன்ற சாயலும், இற் பிறப்பும்,
பக்கத்தார் பாராட்டப் பாடு எய்தும்; தான் உரைப்பின்,
மைத்துனர் பல்கி, 'மருந்தின் தணியாத
பித்தன்!' என்று எள்ளப்படும்.

Chapter 35 - Inferior baseness
***

Men of lower calibre will never improve even if their status in elevated. The congenital quality of such people cannot be transformed overnight. The quality of such low – level people is enumerated in the following ten stanzas

341. As a hen never stops clawing of garbage
     Though nice granules of rice are put near its beak;
     Even when cerebral volumes are explained to them
     Base - minded fellows behave whimsically.

Cerebral volumes are those that are deep in contents and thought-provoking. Even if anything worthwhile is taught to them, the base-minded persons will not pay heed to it but behave in any manner they like.

> கப்பி கடவதாக் காலைத் தன் வாய்ப் பெயினும்,
> குப்பை கிளைப்பு ஓவாக் கோழிபோல், மிக்க
> கனம் பொதிந்த நூல் விரித்துக் காட்டினும், கீழ் தன்
> மனம் புரிந்தவாறே மிகும்.

342. If it is advised that with noble principles
     We will align with immaculate great men,
     Lower man will get up saying, 'We will go to sleep;
     Also by putting some excuse, he will go away.

If a learned man attempts to reform an inferior person, he would not follow the guidelines but will side-track the issue and go off in his own way. Persons of inferior quality will never improve.

> 'காழ் ஆய கொண்டு, கசடு அற்றார்தம் சாரல்,
> தாழாது போவாம்' என உரைப்பின், கீழ்தான்,
> 'உறங்குவாம்' என்று எழுந்து போமாம்; அஃது அன்றி,
> மறங்குமாம், மற்று ஒன்று உரைத்து.

343. Ye, Lord of a country of perennial cascades! Great
Men of learning, even after becoming rich would be
Of high calibre, unwavering; when inferior becomes
Rich, he would be one step different in his behaviour.

Great men of richness, will be unwavering in their noble qualities of humbleness, charity and kindness. But inferior fellows, when becoming rich will be proud and haughty.

பெரு நடை தாம் பெறினும், பெற்றி பிழையாது
ஒரு நடையார் ஆகுவர், சான்றோர்; பெரு நடை
பெற்றக்கடைத்தும்,-பிறங்கு அருவி நல் நாட!-
வற்று ஆம் ஒரு நடை, கீழ்.

344. Ye, Lord of a country of great cascades! Great
Men would consider even an iota of help done by
Others as gigantic; but even when such huge help
Is done, inferior low fellows will never realize it.

Low - level inferior men will be notorious for their ingratitude but really great people will be reputed for their nobility of gratitude. In the Tamil original, the measure of help is exemplified as *Tinai* and *Panai,* the grain (millet) and a tall palm tree. Rhyming words of the original defy translation and hence *tinai* and *panai* are replaced by iota and gigantic in the English version.

திணை அனைத்தே ஆயினும் செய்த நன்று உண்டால்,
பனை அனைத்தா உள்ளுவர், சான்றோர்; பனை அனைத்து
என்றும் செயினும்,-இலங்கு அருவி நல் நாட!
நன்று இல, நன்று அறியார்மாட்டு.

345. Though fed in a golden tray, a dog would
Keenly look for waste-food without winking
Its eyes; likewise, even if an ill – bred is
Highly respected, his will be a deviant behavior.

If people of low calibre are given dignified role in life, they would behave differently and betray their base mentality.

> பொற்கலத்து ஊட்டிப் புறந்தரினும், நாய் பிறர்
> எச்சிற்கு இமையாது பார்த்திருக்கும்; அச் சீர்,
> பெருமை உடைத்தாக் கொளினும், கீழ் செய்யும்
> கருமங்கள் வேறுபடும்.

346. If great men acquire royal wealth, never
     In life will they speak excessive words; but
     When low-bred gets a lot of wealth from
     A minimum, he thinks of himself as Great Indhran.

Moderate humbleness of great men and an intemperate haughtiness of low-bred are juxtaposed in this stanza. God Indhra is the ruler of golden paradise.

Lot of wealth is indicated as *Kaani* and *minimum* is noted as *munthiri* in the Tamil original. They were the technical terms to denote the extent of ground space.

> சக்கரச் செல்வம் பெறினும், விழுமியோர்
> எக் காலும் சொல்லார் மிகுதிச்சொல்; எக் காலும்
> முந்திரிமேற் காணி மிகுவதேல், கீழ் தன்னை
> இந்திரனா எண்ணிவிடும்.

347. Though made of pure gold studded with gems
     Sandals are meant for one's own feet; likewise
     Low - bred men, even though huge wealthy, will be
     Identified with what actions they perform.

Ill – bred men will indulge in undesirable activities, even if they become enormously wealthy. They will be identified of their low calibre with their behavior and activities. It shall be noticed that the last two lines of this stanza are found in stanza - 350 also. May be both the Tamil poems are authored by one and the same person.

ம தீர் பசும் பொன்மேல் மாண்ட மணி அழுத்திச்
செய்தது எனினும், செருப்புத் தன் கார்க்கே ஆம்;-
எய்திய செல்வத்தர் ஆயினும், கீழ்களைச்
செய் தொழிலால் காணப்படும்.

348. Ye, Lord of great hills! Men of low calibre are
Of harsh verbosity, devoid of mercy and love
Elated at the misery of others, being impatient
Feeling agitated and mockingly speaking of others.

All these undesirable tendencies are found among the persons of low calibre. Hence the stanza implies that these have to be avoided by decent persons in their day to day life.

கடுக்கெனச் சொல்வற்று ஆம்; கண்ணோட்டம் இன்றாம்;
இடுக்கண் பிறர்மாட்டு உவக்கும்; அடுத்து அடுத்து
வேகம் உடைத்து ஆம்; விறல் மலை நல் நாட!
ஏகுமாம்; எள்ளுமாம்; கீழ்.

349. Ye, Lord of resounding sea-shores with honey -
dripping *Neithal*
Flowers! If one stands behind the great for
Many days, they will treat him kindly for old
Friendship; but persons of low caliber will
dishonour him.

Men of inferior variety set aside even those who moved with friendliness for many days in the past. But great men will behave with love and affection, especially to those who are already familiar with them.

'பழையர் இவர்' என்று பல்நாள் பின் நிற்பின்,
உழை இனியர் ஆகுவர், சான்றோர்; விழையாதே,
கள் உயிர்க்கும் நெய்தல் கனை கடல் தண் சேர்ப்ப!
எள்ளுவர், கீழாயவர்.

350. Listen, my dear! Young calves can't be
 Yoked to chariots, even when feeding daily with
 Tender grass, low-bred men, though rich
 Will be identified with the actions they perform.

Though richly fed, young calves will not be of use to draw chariots. Similarly, ignoble men will be of no use to others, even when they become rich.

கொய் புல் கொடுத்துக் குறைத்து என்றும் தீற்றினும்,
வையம் பூண்கல்லா, சிறு குண்டை;-ஐய! கேள்;
எய்திய செல்வத்தர் ஆயினும், கீழ்களைச்
செய்தொழிலால் காணப்படும்.

Chapter 36 - Viciousness
***

Absence of virtue is almost a viciousness. It is a quality that borders foolishness also. This theme has already been dealt with in the previous chapter. But still it continues in the following stanzas.

351. Great and wise persons, though young, safeguard
     And control themselves well; Lower beings
     Of little knowledge do vicious deeds as they grow
     Roam about like vultures and remain guilty.

Knowledgeable persons, even though young in age control their senses and safeguard themselves without any blemishes. Men of lower calibre, as they grow continue to do evil deeds and roam about like carrion - eating vultures.

ஆர்த்த அறிவினர், ஆண்டு இளையர் ஆயினும்,
காத்து ஓம்பித் தம்மை அடக்குப; மூத்தொறூஉம்
தீத்தொழிலே கன்றித் திரிதந்து, எருவைபோல்
போத்து அறார், புல்லறிவினார்.

352. Frogs are incapable of erasing scum 'from their
     Glossy skin, though live in expansive ponds, as
     The unwise men are unable to comprehend the finer
     Aspects of best treatises, even after reading them.

As frogs are incapable of removing the slippery dirt from their skin even though they live in water, men of poor knowledge are not able to understand the depth and intricacies of reputed treatises even after reading them.

செழும் பெரும் பொய்கையுள் வாழினும், என்றும்
வழும்பு அறுக்கில்லாவாம், தேரை; வழும்பு இல் சீர்
நூல் கற்றக்கண்ணும், நுணுக்கம் ஒன்று இல்லாதார்
தேர்கிற்கும் பெற்றி அரிது.

353. Ye, Lord of a row of hills! Very rare for great
Men to speak of even others' virtues in absence;
But to speak in person, falsely of others' qualities
With what ill-bred men's tongue has been made of?

Even to do a good think of speaking good of others in their absence, great men would be hesitant. But men of lower level would speak falsely of others even in their very presence. To speak derogatively, unmindful of injuring the feeling of others, and that too in their presence, with what that ill-bred man's tongue was made of, the poet wonders.

கண மலை நல் நாட!-கண் இன்று ஒருவர்
குணனேயும் கூறற்கு அரிதால்; குணன் அழுங்கக்
குற்றம் உழை நின்று கூறும் சிறியவர்கட்கு
எற்றால் இயன்றதோ, நா!

354. Domestic ladies of hairy wide vaginal organs
Would not parade their feminine grace as
Whores; but prostitutes, as speedily as fresh flood
Proudly put on to decorate excessively.

What the poem implies is that great women would never indulge in professing their talent, however much they are capable. But stupid lower elements will speak of themselves very highly even though they are not that much knowledgeable.

கோடு ஏந்து அகல் அல்குல் பெண்டிர் தம் பெண் நீர்மை
சேடியர் போலச் செயல் தேற்றார்; கூடி,
புதுப்பெருக்கம் போலத் தம் பெண் நீர்மை காட்டி,
மதித்து இறப்பர், மற்றையவர்.

355. Low-men are like a chisel that never
 Pierce through even a tender leaf unless hit it;
 Never do any help for indigent; but do all help
 To those who are meant to hit and harm them.

Men of low qualities would not do anything good by themselves. If some violent man spurred them on into action, they would function. Unless they are hurt, they wouldn't do anything good.

> தளிர்மேலே நிற்பினும், தட்டாமல் செல்லா
> உளி நீரர் மாதோ, கயவர்; அளி நீரார்க்கு
> என்னானும் செய்யார்; எனைத்தானும் செய்பவே,
> இன்னாங்கு செய்வார்ப் பெறின்.

356. A tribe would think of hill's welfare;
 A peasant would think of field's harvest;
 Higher-ups would remember of good deeds of others;
 A Low-bred would think of the abuse of others.

By thinking of abuse of others, they would be mindful of doing harm to others. Inherent quality of the men of low calibre is put on comparison with those of others.

> மலை நலம் உள்ளும், குறவன்; பயந்த
> விளை நிலம் உள்ளும், உழவன்; சிறந்து ஒருவர்
> செய்த நன்று உள்ளுவர் சான்றோர்; கயம், தன்னை
> வைததை உள்ளிவிடும்.

357. Even if offences hundred done by a person
 Who did one good, great men would pardon him;
 Despite having done seven hundred good but if one
 Is fallible, ill bred would deem the entire hundreds bad.

What is explained in this stanza is the toleration of great people and the ill-tempered nature of low-level persons.

ஒரு நன்றி செய்தவர்க்கு ஒன்றி எழுந்த
பிழை நூறும் சான்றோர் பொறுப்பர்; கயவர்க்கு
எழுநூறு நன்றி செய்து, ஒன்று தீதுஆயின்,
எழுநூறும் தீதாய்விடும்.

358. Ye! bright - eyed damsel ! Even if swine
Is adorned with jewel, won't be an elephant;
Likewise, what men born of great families do during
Poverty, fools wouldn't do even in their prosperity.

The stinginess of the fools and the generosity of great men are explained here. Comparable is the content of stanza-149 and of 184.

ஏட்டைப் பருவத்தும் இற் பிறந்தார் செய்வன,
மோட்டிடத்தும் செய்யார், முழுமக்கள்;-கோட்டை
வயிரம் செறிப்பினும்,-வாள் கண்ணாய்!-பன்றி
செயிர் வேழம் ஆகுதல் இன்று.

359. Many low-bred men thinking 'now I become
Rich, a bit after wards, and felt glad with
These words in mind but in a changed manner later
Find them died, as if lotus leaf dried off in a pond.

Men of lower calibre build castles in the air that they would develop their wealth, saying - today, tomorrow and in the near future. Without doing anything good with what they have, they breathe their last. Their uncertain life is aptly compared to lotus – leaf which will be alive so long as water remains in the pond. Then it dies of its own. The implication is that men should do some charity sooner than later. Doing good should not be postponed on some pretext or other.

'இன்று ஆதும்; இந் நிலையே ஆதும்; இனிச் சிறிது
நின்று ஆதும்' என்று நினைத்திருந்து, ஒன்றி
உரையின் மகிழ்ந்து, தம் உள்ளம் வேறு ஆகி,
மரை இலையின் மாய்ந்தார், பலர்.

360. Though born in water, lush green in colour,
 Pith has no moisture in it and likewise
 Though fabulously wealthy, there are men
 In the world, merciless and as hard as rocky stone.

Not all wealthy people are generous. Generosity is a great virtue. Possessing wealth does not make a man generous. This miserliness is compared to a pith, which has no moisture even though it grows in the water itself.

நீருள் பிறந்து, நிறம் பசியதுஆயினும்,
ஈரம் கிடையகத்து இல் ஆகும்;-ஒரும்
நிறைப் பெருஞ் செல்வத்து நின்றக்கடைத்தும்,
அறைப் பெருங்கல் அன்னார் உடைத்து.

Chapter 37 - Miscellany of ethics
***

Padhumanaar who classified the four hundred poems of Naaladiyaar has chosen a lot of miscellaneous poems that cannot be grouped in the thirty six foregone chapters. It is these poems of independent themes is listed out herein. Variety of ethical points that are not connected with one another are dealt with here.

361. No use of his house if the person doesn't have a
  Highly respectable wife even if the house has, sky -
  high
  Towers with special fortifying walls illuminated by
  lamps;
  Also it is alike wild forest undeserving to be seen.

However much a man is wealthy, it is of no use if he doesn't have a highly respectable wife. His house will be splendid if only he has his virtuous wife there. Otherwise that house is comparable to wild forest, the poet says.

மழை திளைக்கும் மாடம் ஆய், மாண்பு அமைந்த காப்பு ஆய்,
இழை விளக்கு நின்று இமைப்பின் என் ஆம், விழைதக்க
மாண்ட மனையாளை இல்லாதான் இல்லகம்?
காண்டற்கு அரியது ஓர் காடு!

362. Despite unmistakable custody of swordsmen
  If women of few words are found in guilt,
  Few are their days of not having done it;
  More is the duration of having done it.

What the poem implies is that even if there is a vigilance and guard, the immorality of certain women cannot be prevented. Morality will be safe guarded if only they are good in behavior and at heart. Compare the content of Kural-57 that speaks about the virtues of wife.

> வழுக்கு எனைத்தும் இல்லாத வாள்வாய்க் கிடந்தும்,
> இழுக்கினைத் தாம் பெறுவர் ஆயின், இழுக்கு எனைத்தும்
> செய்குறாப் பாணி சிறிதே, அச் சின்மொழியார்
> கை உறாப் பாணி பெரிது.

363. One who defy and confront is like God of death;
Incurable disease if absent in kitchen in the morn;
One who doesn't serve cooked food is like a ghost;
These wives are weapons to kill husbands.

Quality of three types of women is enumerated in this stanza. This poem reflects the trend prevailed in Tamil Nadu hundreds of years ago. When modern feminism is highlighted at present, men are expected to share what all women are meant to do except pregnancy and delivery. John Milton says, *Nothing lovelier to be found among women than to do household duties and promote the arts of husbandry.* Paradise Lost Book IX.

> 'எறி' என்று எதிர் நிற்பாள் கூற்றம்; சிறுகாலை
> அட்டில் புகாதாள் அரும் பிணி; அட்டதனை
> உண்டி உதவாதாள் இல் வாழ் பேய்;-இம் மூவர்
> கொண்டானைக் கொல்லும் படை.

364. Having heard to end up domestic chores
He doesn't; even after harsh sound of death knell
Doesn't realize but infatuated with one more wife
Are all offences deserve him to be pelted with stones.

This stanza attempts to inform the householders about the importance of renunciation. When the wife expires, many widowers get married. Worse still, there are many who live with one more wife, official or un official. This is also condemned in this stanza. Pelting a guilty man with stones seems to have been a socially accepted punishment in those days. Some Gulf countries like Saudi Arabia still practise it as a rule of Shariat law.

> 'கடி' எனக் கேட்டும், கடியான்; வெடிபட
> ஆர்ப்பது கேட்டும், அது தெளியான்; பேர்த்தும் ஓர்
> இல் கொண்டு இனிது இருஉம் ஏழுறுதல், என்பவே,
> கல் கொண்டு எறியும் தவறு.

365. Excellent it is to attempt to live as ascetic;
 Life with pleasant wife in household is mediocre;
 Hoping to get and go avariciously behind another
 Who doesn't recognize you is the lowest of all in life.

Leading a life of renunciation is the best; a life with one's own wife in domestic bliss is the next in category. The worst in this list is one's behaviour of going behind greedily to get favours from another who doesn't even recognize him.

> தலையே, தவம் முயன்று வாழ்தல்; ஒருவர்க்கு
> இடையே, இனியார்கண் தங்கல்; கடையே,
> புணராது என்று எண்ணிப் பொருள் நசையால், தம்மை
> உணரார் பின் சென்று நிலை.

366. Persons spending time in reading are the top - most;
 Those enjoy benevolent in life are in middle;
                                                                      ambitiously
 Asserting and remain sleepless saying not yet eaten
 Well, nor earning well – are in the lowest of low levels.

Greediness is condemned but reading and leading a domestic are not only highlighted but even appreciated. It may be recalled that Francis Bacon in his *Essays* has allotted, a chapter on *Reading* which is worth comparable. Neither greedy nor stingy but those who lead a normal life are better. Worst are those who are ambitious and unsatisfied.

கல்லாக் கழிப்பர், தலையாயார், நல்லவை
துவ்வாக் கழிப்பர், இடைகள்; கடைகள்,
'இனிது உண்ணேம்! ஆரப் பெறேம் யாம்!' என்னும்
முனிவினால் கண்பாடு இலர்.

368. Ye, the peasant of a place that yields rich
Harvest of paddy! As sprouts germinate from paddy
Again grow into same paddy seeds in plenty during
Harvest, genius of the son is the genius of the father!

This is only a probability. No guarantee that all the sons born of a father are typically intelligent as their father. Exceptions are there in plenty.

செந்நெல்லால் ஆய செழு முளை மற்றும் அச்
செந்நெல்லே ஆகி விளைதலால்,-அந் நெல்
வயல் நிறையக் காய்க்கும் வள வயல் ஊர!
மகன் அறிவு, தந்தை அறிவு.

368. Men of huge wealth and fame get spoiled
But children of concubines and low-bred get richer
Displaying world's nature where top goes to bottom
And vice versa as the top-stem of an umbrella.

High and low in any walk of life are changeable, not permanent. All depending upon one's own destiny. Not desirable therefore for rich men to be proud and poor men to be embittered. Wheel of fortune is constantly rotating to give room for poor to become rich and rich to become poor. One has to put up with these ups and downs in life.

உடைப் பெருஞ் செல்வரும் சான்றோரும் கெட்டு,
புடைப் பெண்டிர் மக்களும் கீழும் பெருகி,
கடைக்கால் தலைக்கண்ணது ஆகி, குடைக் கால்போல்
கீழ் மேலாய் நிற்கும், உலகு!

369. Ye! Lord of hills and of falls that scatter stones!
Men with no mercy to eliminate the ills of close
Friends even when they report it for redressal
May die of a fall from hill rather than being alive.

Not eliminating the suffering of endearing friends even when they report it for redressal, is not desirable for friends of olden days. They should go in for redressing their grievances.

> இனியார் தம் நெஞ்சத்து நோய் உரைப்ப, அந் நோய்
> தணியாத உள்ளம் உடையார்,-மணி வரன்றி
> வீழும் அருவி விறல் மலை நல் நாட!
> வாழ்வின், வரை பாய்தல் நன்று.

370. Swelling flood and intimacy of whores of ear-rings
On a scrutiny are found not to be different from
One another water recedes when rain stops;
Whore's love wears off if customer stops money.

Unreliability of prostitutes is pointed out here. Their intimacy is in proportion to the money given by her paramour. When he stops money, she slips away as water recedes when rain stops.

> புதுப் புனலும், பூங்குழையார் நட்பும், இரண்டும்,
> விதுப்பு அற நாடின், வேறு அல்ல;-புதுப் புனலும்
> மாரி அறவே அறுமே; அவர் அன்பும்
> வாரி அறவே அறும்.

Chapter 38 – Prostitutes
***

A prostitute does not belong to one person. Indiscriminately to those who offer money, the prostitutes render their physical frame to be enjoyed. Hence they are treated ignobly in literature and in life. Following stanzas elaborate on this theme. Mostly in western countries, prostitution is legalized and recognized as a profession. This is to ensure hygiene in the trade and to avoid nefarious trickery of pimps.

371. Brightness of lamps and friendship of whores
 Are not different, if looked at deeply; brightness
 Will fade when ghee is dried; so too disappear
 The passion of whores when paramour stops money.

The poem implies that the false passion of a prostitute is not as genuine as that of a conjugal love and of the wife. Hence that alone is real and enjoyable.

விளக்கு ஒளியும், வேசையர் நட்பும், இரண்டும்,
துளக்கு அற நாடின், வேறு அல்ல;-விளக்கு ஒளியும்
நெய் அற்றகண்ணே அறுமே; அவர் அன்பும்
கை அற்றகண்ணே அறும்.

372. A whore of hairy organ and chosen jewels, said once
 We both will fall off precipice, if need be but at present
 Since I have no money she on the pretext of palsy in
 leg, wept
 And went off without coming to the peak.

The poem reads like a story of a man who bemoans the way he was cheated. What the poem implies is that real love is one that emerges from one's own housewife and not from prostitutes.

அம் கோட்டு அகல் அல்குல் ஆய் இழையாள், நம்மொடு,
'செங்கோடு பாய்துமே' என்றாள்மன்; செங் கோட்டின்
மேல் காணம் இன்மையால் மேவாது ஒழிந்தாளே,
கால் கால்நோய் காட்டிக் கழுழ்ந்து.

373. Let him even be the red-eyed *God Thirumal*
Who is revered by beings of celestial world;
The whores of tender and soft bodies would
Pray and send out those who have nothing to offer.

Prostitutes will never consider either the greatness or the beauty of men. They will cohabit with anybody who gives money. If no money, they will send him out. Hence the love from them is only a pretence and not genuine and reliable.

அம் கண் விசும்பின் அமரர் தொழப்படும்
செங் கண் மால் ஆயினும் ஆகமன்! தம் கைக்
கொடுப்பது ஒன்று இல்லாரை, கொய் தளிர் அன்னார்,
விடுப்பர், தம் கையால் தொழுது.

374. To analyse the blue – lily eyed whores of
Loveless mind, money-less men are alike poison
To them; men with huge money, even if they are
Dirty oil -mongers are as sweet as sugar to them.

Abhorrent is the company of prostitutes who are neither faithful nor believable. They are after money and money only.

ஆணம் இல் நெஞ்சத்து அணி நீலக் கண்ணார்க்குக்
காணம் இல்லாதார் கடு அனையர்;-காணவே
செக்கு ஊர்ந்து கொண்டானும் செய்த பொருள் உடையார்
அக்காரம் அன்னார், அவர்க்கு.

375. Beastly fools are those who sleep with prostitutes
Who are like elusive eels that deceitfully
Show their head - side to snakes and tail-end
To fishes that live in pellucid ponds of water.

Eel is a long thin fish that looks like a snake but it is edible. Its nature is such that it neither aligns with snakes nor with fishes. Similarly prostitutes are neither faithful to A who comes in the morning nor to B who comes in the evening. Hence they are compared to eels that are elusive and slippery.

> பாம்பிற்கு ஒரு தலை காட்டி, ஒரு தலை
> தேம் படு தெண் கயத்து மீன் காட்டும் ஆங்கு
> மலங்கு அன்ன செய்கை மகளிர் தோள் சேர்வர்,
> விலங்கு அன்ன வெள்ளறிவினார்.

376. The gold-bangled whore, assured of living as one
 As perforated gems and their thread and as undivided
 Anril birds, has now twisted herself as a fighting ram's horn;
 Oh! My mind ! do you still go to her? Or come along with me!

A customer feels dejected at the ingratitude of a prostitute and vexedly asking this question to his mind. What this stanza implies is that nobody should believe the prostitutes. Not known whether the bird 'anril' ever lived in the world. May be a fabulous bird. But invariably celebrated in Tamil literature as a species of undivided love.

> 'பொத்த நூல் கல்லும், புணர் பிரியா அன்றிலும்போல்,
> நித்தலும் நம்மைப் பிரியலம்' என்று உரைத்த
> பொற்றொடியும் போர்த் தகர்க் கோடு ஆயினாள்; நல் நெஞ்சே!
> நிற்றியோ, போதியோ, நீ?

377. After giving caressing comfort as a wild cow,
 Whores squeeze away the wealth and lie down
 As buffalo; men who complacently believed
 Their false love will get disgraced at length.

Any relationship with prostitutes will bring loss and dishonor and the happiness they provide seasonally will result in a great dishonour.

> ஆமாபோல் நக்கி, அவர் கைப் பொருள் கொண்டு,
> சேமாப்போல் குப்புறூஉம் சில்லைக்கண் அன்பினை
> ஏமாந்து, எமது என்று இருந்தார் பெறுபவே,
> தாமாம் பலரால் நகை.

378. Adherents to morality would be abhorring bulky
 Breasts of deer-eyed damsels, as they have a
 ram's
 Mind twisted to persons in indigence, though
 once
 Moved with them sweetly in their richness.

Hence great men realize that whore's company is unbelievable and they would not go near her. Men of ignorance, perhaps unaware of the nature of whores get into their company and suffer subsequently.

> ஏமாந்த போழ்தின் இனியார் போன்று, இன்னாராய்த்
> தாம் ஆர்ந்த போதே தகர்க்கோடு ஆம், மான் நோக்கின்,
> தம் நெறிப் பெண்டிர் தட முலை சேராரே-
> 'செந் நெறிச் சேர்தும்' என்பார்.

379. Bright faced whores hide their vicious mind;
 Having heard and believed their credulous words,
 Let the gullible think that they are theirs; fact is
 Whores are kins to none but to their bodies only.

Prostitutes are hypocrites; they pretend to show their love, so long as one pays handsomely. They believe that their bodies are their assets. Hence, It is absolute foolishness to believe them.

> ஊறு செய் நெஞ்சம் தம் உள் அடக்கி, ஒண்ணுதலார்
> தேற மொழிந்த மொழி கேட்டு, தேறி,
> 'எமர்' என்று கொள்வாரும் கொள்பவே; யார்க்கும்
> தமர் அல்லர்; தம் உடம்பினார்.

380. Though known that bright – faced whores
 Keep their mind fixed with one but move
 with their cunning actions, persons of sinful
 Deeds do not seem to have realized it.

Whores move with one but their mind will hover around another. Whores move with one but their mind will hover around another. Well known it is that among prostitutes, speech differ from actions and vice versa. But still men of sinful actions do not seem to have realized it.

உள்ளம் ஒருவன் உழையதா, ஒண்ணுதலார்
கள்ளத்தால் செய்யும் கருத்து எல்லாம் தெள்ளி
அறிந்த இடத்தும், அறியாராம்-பாவம்
செறிந்த உடம்பினவர்.

Chapter 39 - Women of Chastity
***

It is a pity that chastity mostly in western culture has already gone out-moded and this tendency is slowly getting into oriental countries also. At one stage, chastity was insisted not for women only but also for men. This was not only understandable but certainly agreeable also. But the present trend is the very concept of chastity is questioned. This is the way of life in modern days. But what the following stanzas say is only a replica of what prevailed hundreds of years ago in Tamil Nadu. However the first six poems enumerate the virtuous qualities of household women.

381. Though famed as *Ayiranee* of rare chastity
A fair lady who is protective of behaving that
Nobody with a carnal mind stands behind
Her, is a benevolent better - half to a man.

Ayiranee is the wife God *Indhiran*. She is also known as *Indhirani* for women; being reputed as *Indhirani* is not enough. A lady must behave and protect herself in such a way that no man with a sexual intention should stand behind her. That woman alone will prove to be a good housewife.

> அரும் பெறல் கற்பின் அயிராணி அன்ன
> பெரும் பெயர்ப் பெண்டிர் எனினும், விரும்பிப்
> பெறு நசையால், பின்நிற்பார் இன்மையே பேணும்
> நறு நுதலாள்-நன்மைத் துணை.

382. Even at the suffering of drinking boiled water
Only or when ocean - like large number of guests
Arrive, the one who is pleasant and behave virtuously
Is a woman eminently fit for a family life.

Persons who suffer acute poverty will try to survive by drinking boiled water. Even in the days of such poverty, one who doesn't deviate from virtuous deeds and pleasant behavior is a suitable woman for household life.

> குட நீர் அட்டு உண்ணும் இடுக்கண் பொழுதும்,
> கடல் நீர் அற உண்ணும் கேளிர் வரினும்,
> கடன் நீர்மை கையாறாக் கொள்ளும் மட மொழி
> மாதர்-மனை மாட்சியாள்.

383. A house is the best if only the wife is dutiful
    Chaste and reputable to be honoured by her village;
    Though that house is little in size, broken on four
    Sides and gives way for rains to pour down into it.

Even in extreme poverty, a wife in the household is meant to be tolerant, chaste and reputable. This appears to be too much for a woman to bear. The poem as such is absolutely silent about the duties of the male householder. Can this be charitable on his part to leave the lady alone to suffer is a question to be answered.

> நால் ஆறும் ஆறாய், நனி சிறிதாய், எப் புறனும்
> மேல் ஆறு மேல் உறை சோரினும், மேலாய
> வல்லாளாய், வாழும் ஊர் தற் புகழும் மாண் கற்பின்
> இல்லாள் அமைந்ததே-இல்.

384. Pleasant to her husband, decorate to his taste
    Timid and shy to others in village, fearful of him
    Feigned disliking and then enrapturing him with
    Words virtuous, is a woman fit to be a housewife.

One wonders whether half of such regulations and norms are prescribed for men in the societal set up of the Tamilians.

> கட்கு இனியாள், காதலன் காதல் வகை புனைவாள்
> உட்கு உடையாள், ஊராண் இயல்பினாள், உட்கி
> இடன் அறிந்து ஊடி இனிதின் உணரும்
> மடமொழி மாதராள்-பெண்.

385. Shy we are as if we knew the comfort then only
 Though my husband caresses my shoulders daily;
 How did whores feel when, prompted by a greed
 For money embrace the chests of various men?

This poem is purported to have been addressed by a modest wife. She is attributing dishonour to prostitutes; also mocks at their pluralistic behaviour and the character of whores.

> எஞ்ஞான்றும், எம் கணவர் எம் தோள்மேல் சேர்ந்து எழினும்,
> அஞ் ஞான்று கண்டேம்போல் நாணுதுமால்; எஞ்ஞான்றும்,
> என்னை, கெழீஇயினர் கொல்லோ, பொருள் நசையால்
> பல் மார்பு சேர்ந்து ஒழுகுவார்!

386. Beauty of a modest housewife is like a treatise
 Studied well by a scholar, a treasure in the hands of a
 Charitable person and also like a
 Sharp sword in the hands of a brave warrior.

Implication of this stanza is that both the best wealth and an eminent treatise are highly benevolent. Beauty of a modest housewife and the sharp sword in the hands of a hero are unapproachable by others.

> உள்ளத்து உணர்வுடையான் ஓதிய நூல் அற்றால்;
> வள்ளன்மை பூண்டான்கண் ஒண் பொருள்; தெள்ளிய
> ஆண்மகன் கையில் அயில் வாள் அனைத்துஅரோ;-
> நாணுடையாள் பெற்ற நலம்.

387. A ruralite is said to have bought a mix of horse gram
 Of black and red together; likewise the broad-chested
 Husband of mine, having hugged already a whore
 Comes to me, to embrace, devoid of bathing.

Like a rural peasant who doesn't discriminate red gram from that of black, my husband treats me indiscriminately of a prostitute. Not only the physical hygiene is a core - point but also the modest accusation of a housewife towards her husband's illegal and clandestinely done immoral activity with a prostitute.

> கருங் கொள்ளும், செங் கொள்ளும், தூணிப் பதக்கு என்று
> ஒருங்கு ஒப்பக் கொண்டானாம், ஊரன்;-ஒருங்கு ஒவ்வா
> நல் நுதலார்த் தோய்ந்த வரைமார்பன் நீராடாது,
> என்னையும் தோய வரும்!

388. Oh! Bard, don't say the cruel words to me; I serve
No purpose to the Lord like the left side of a drum;
If want to say, withdraw slowly and say this to
Another whore who is like right side of the drum.

The cruel words are those that indicate the likely visit of husband to a prostitute. The poem is addressed to a bard who has a duty to mollify the ire of a good housewife. He has been deputed by the husband to his lady. She is angry because, he has violated the decency of a good husband by his romantic visit to a prostitute. The housewife says that the news of her husband's returning or otherwise may be communicated to another whore to whom he might even go again.

> கொடியவை கூறாதி;-பாண!-நீ கூறின்,
> அடி பைய இட்டு ஒதுங்கிச் சென்று, துடியின்
> இடக்கண் அனையம் யாம், ஊரற்கு; அதனால்,
> வலக் கண் அனையார்க்கு உரை.

389. I once didn't brook flying of flea on my lord
Of a place where water springs in fields after uprooting
Steep grass; again now I simply look at his perfumed
Chest after having hotly dashed with whore's breast.

The housewife sorrowfully reports to her maid servant that she is unable to control the licentiousness of her husband. It is she who did not brook even the disturbance of a flea of him once. I simply tolerate his unholy friendship with a whore, now.

சாய்ப் பறிக்க நீர் திகழும் தண் வயல் ஊரன்மீது
ஈப் பறக்க நொந்தேனும் யானேமன்! தீப் பறக்கத்
தாக்கி முலை பொருத தண் சாந்து அணி அகலம்
நோக்கி இருந்தேனும் யான்!

390. Ye, bard! Don't tell me a lie that my lord of a
Garland of matured buds would be merciful to me;
I become bitter to him as the top of sugarcane;
Tell the whores who are sweet to him as the middle
– joint.

This was addressed by a housewife to the bard who has come to intercede with her on behalf of her erroneous husband.

'அரும்பு அவிழ் தாரினான் எம் அருளும்' என்று
பெரும் பொய் உரையாதி;-பாண!-கரும்பின்
கடைக் கண் அனையம் யாம் ஊரற்கு; அதனால்,
இடைக் கண் அனையார்க்கு உரை.

Chapter 40 - Expression of love
***

Love and lust are closer to one another but different in concept. Lust is enforced and violent. Love is tender, soft and genuine. Genuine love is depicted in various methods. A romantic pleasure enjoyed by the couple is more for enjoying among themselves than for expressing it to others. That is why ancient Tamil literature classified it as a separate unit – *Aham* which means "inside' – something that is to be felt within. The following ten stanzas enumerate the ways and means of enjoying love besides defining its various aspects.

391. Ye, Lord of a long coast of back – waters of roaring
 Waves! Unless the lady co - habits, she will be
 Greenish; if not feel feigned anger, love will be
 Of no taste; so cohabit and have feigned anger.

To enjoy one's own romantic love, both the feigned anger and co-habitation are essential. This stanza is purported to have been said by the maid-servant.

முயங்காக்கால், பாயும் பசலை; மற்று ஊடி
உயங்காக்கால், உப்பு இன்றாம் காமம்;-வயங்கு ஓதம்
நில்லாத் திரை அலைக்கும் நீள் கழித் தண் சேர்ப்ப!-
புல்லாப் புலப்பது ஓர் ஆறு.

392. Lord's separation to the love – lorn ladies who
 Delightfully hugged their garlanded chest on days
 Thunder in all directions in the rainy season
 Appears to be the tolling of death - knell.

The lover is away on duty. He is yet to come. His separation is unbearable to the lady in the main session. Her pangs of anxiety is expressed in this stanza.

தம் அமர் காதலர் தார் சூழ் அணி அகலம்
விம்ம முயங்கும் துணை இல்லார்க்கு, இம்மெனப்
பெய்ய எழிலி முழங்கும் திசைஎல்லாம்
நெய்தல் அறைந்தன்ன நீர்த்து.

393. A wife who makes garland of chosen flowers
In the weariedevening when blacksmiths downed
Their gadgets, asking herself 'what benefit this
Garland is to render and then threw it on the ground.

Her dejection in mind and rejection of garland are due to her information that her husband is shortly to leave her on some essential duty. This separation is unbearable and that is why she throws down the garland in bitterness and disgust.

கம்மம் செய் மாக்கள் கருவி ஒடுக்கிய
மம்மர் கொள் மாலை, மலர் ஆய்ந்து, பூத் தொடுப்பாள்,
கைம் மாலை இட்டுக் கலுழ்ந்தாள், 'துணை இல்லார்க்கு
இம் மாலை என் செய்வது!' என்று.

394. Gazing at the setting sun and gently wiping
Off tears from her red hued eyes, despondingly
Wept, marking the day with her soft finger and
Sleeplessly down with arms at her pillow, thinking
me of guilty.

This is what the Lord says to his charioteer whether the lady at home will be thinking of himself as guilty for not having returned early from his avocations elsewhere.

செல் சுடர் நோக்கிச் சிதர் அரிக் கண் கொண்ட நீர்
மெல் விரல் ஊழ் தெறியா, விம்மி, தன் மெல் விரலின்,
நாள் வைத்து, நம் குற்றம் எண்ணும்கொல், அந்தோ! தன்
தோள் வைத்து அணைமேல் கிடந்து!

395. Kingfisher followed my lady thinking of her
 Eyes as fishes; and still attempted but having
 Seen her comely eye brows are of the shape
 Of a bow, it was not able to peck at them.

This is how the Lord speaks of his lady - love's beauty to his companion. Eyes are like fishes-brows as bows.

> கண் கயல் என்னும் கருத்தினால், காதலி
> பின் சென்றது அம்ம, சிறு சிரல்! பின் சென்றும்,
> ஊக்கி எழுந்தும், எறிகல்லா-ஒண் புருவம்
> கோட்டிய வில் வாக்கு அறிந்து.

396. Lily - like red - mouthed daughter of mine,
 When applying red sponge to beautify her feet,
 She will draw her legs, saying 'be slow, slow,'
 How Such tender feet bear the prickly pebbles of
 the desert?

A Lady has eloped herself with her lover. This combined exit of the lovers is known to her mother a bit late. She bemoans therefore how the girl will bear with the hard and pebble-track of the desert and how she will suffer during the journey.

> அரக்கு ஆம்பல் நாறும் வாய் அம் மருங்கிற்கு, அன்னோ!
> பரற் கானம் ஆற்றின கொல்லோ-அரக்கு ஆர்ந்த
> பஞ்சி கொண்டு ஊட்டினும், 'பையென, பையென!'
> என்று,
> அஞ்சி, பின் வாங்கும் அடி!

397. A lady in separation thought of her lover
 At a red dusky eve, when accounting script
 Writers finish their errand, she wiped off sandal
 Paste from her comely breasts and sobbed.

This report of lady- love's sadness is conveyed by maid – servant to the lover.

ஓலைக் கணக்கர் ஒலி அடங்கு புன் செக்கர்
மாலைப்பொழுதில், மணந்தார் பிரிவு உள்ளி,
மாலை பரிந்திட்டு அழுதாள்-வன முலைமேல்
கோலம் செய் சாந்தம் திமிர்ந்து.

398. Dear bright – bangled maid! You ask if I could
Stride across the rarely passable dry land tomorrow
With my Lord; I could as one who bought a mare
Must have known the ways of riding it also.

This is addressed by a lady – love to her maid, stating that she could gladly walk – along with her lord, unmindful of strenuousness of crossing the dry desert - like area.

' "கடக்க அருங் கானத்து, காளைபின், நாளை
நடக்கவும் வல்லையோ?" என்றி-சுடர்த்தொடீஇ!
பெற்றான் ஒருவன் பெருங் குதிரை அந் நிலையே
கற்றான், அஃது ஊருமாறு?'

399. I wasn't aware why she hugged the breasts'
Nipples, pearl garland and my whole body; it's a
Gesture of my pretty daughter to indicate the plan
Of her trip on a path where deers feared of tigers.

Perhaps a day before day of her exodus with her lover, the lady - love tightly embraced her mother. She didn't understand the significance of it then; belatedly the mother feels sorry for her daughter's fleeing with her lover.

'முலைக்கண்ணும், முத்தும், முழு மெய்யும், புல்லும்
இலக்கணம் யாதும் அறியேன்; கலைக் கணம்
வேங்கை வெரூஉம் நெறி செலிய போலும், என்
பூம்பாவை செய்த குறி.

400. Gold spotted and koengu-buds-like breasted maid!
Three-eyed God Siva, the crow, the hooded snake and
The mother who begot me haven't done me any harm;
But it's the action of my lord to go on earning.

The lady love says that it is the departure of her lover to go out for eking out financial earning has caused her the harm. Not due to my mother-neither due to Manmatha, the instigator of love, koel and Raghu.

This stanza is thick with allusions to indicate Manmatha, Koel and Raaghu who are supposed to heighten the pangs of separation of love – lorn ladies. What the lady implies is that they are not suffering her but her lover's separation is the one that makes her life unpleasant.

> கண் மூன்று உடையானும், காக்கையும், பை அரவும்,
> என் ஈன்ற யாயும், பிழைத்தது என்? பொன் ஈன்ற
> கோங்கு அரும்பு அன்ன முலையாய்! பொருள்வயின்
> பாங்கனார் சென்ற நெறி!

INDEX OF TAMIL POEMS

பாட்டு	பாடல் எண்	பாட்டு	பாடல் எண்
அகத்தாரே	31	ஆமாபோல்	377
அக்கேபோல்	123	ஆர்த்தபொறிய	290
அங்கண்	151	ஆர்த்த அறிவின	351
அங்கண் விசும்பின்	373	ஆவாம் நாம்	32
அங்கோட்டு	372	ஆவேறுருவின	118
அச்சம்	81	ஆற்றும் துணையும்	196
அத்திட்ட	281	ஆன்படுநெய்	238
அடுக்கல்	203	இசைந்த	187
அடைந்தார்ப்	173	இசையாதெனினும்	194
அம்பல்	87	இசையா ஒரு	111
அம்பும்	89	இசையும்	152
அரக்காம்பல்	396	இடம்பட	116
அருகலதாகி	261	இடும்பைகூர்	106
அரும்பவிழ்	390	இட்டாற்றுப்	286
அரும்பெறல்	34	இமைக்கும்	323
அரும்பெறற் கற்பின்	381	இம்மியரிசித்	94
அருளின்	321	இம்மையக்	132
அலகுசால்	140	இம்மையும்	294
அவமதிப்பும்	163	இரவலர்	279
அவ்வியம்	322	இருக்கை	143
அழல்மண்டு	202	இரும்பார்க்கும்	122
அள்ளிக்கொள்	262	இலங்குநீர்த்	226
அறம்புகழ்	82	இல்லம்	53
அறிமின்	172	இல்லாமை	303
அறியாப்பருவத்	171	இல்லாவிடத்தும்	91
அறியாரும்	108	இழித்தக்க	302
அறிவதறிந்	74	இழைத்தநாள்	6
அறுசுவை	1	இளையான்	65
ஆகாதெனின்	336	இறப்பச்சிறி	99
ஆட்கோடாகி	192	இறப்ப நினை	174
ஆட்பார்த்து	20	இறப்பவே	223
ஆணமில்	374	இற்சார்வின்	182

பாட்டு	பாடல் எண்	பாட்டு	பாடல் எண்
இற்பிறப்பில்லார்	320	உறற்பால	103
இற்பிறப்பெண்ணி	212	உறுபுலி	193
இனம்நன்மை	146	உறுபுனல்	185
இனியார்த்தம்	369	உறைப்பரும்	184
இன்பம்	79	ஊக்கித்தாம்	57
இன்றாதும்	360	ஊர் அங்கணம்நீர்	175
இன்றுகொல்	36	ஊருள்	90
இன்னார் இனையர்	205	ஊறிஉவர்த்	47
இன்னா செயின்	76	ஊறுசெய்	379
இன்னா விடுதற்	225	எஞ்ஞான்றும்	385
இன்னா இயைக	305	எத்துணை	272
ஈட்டலும்	280	எந்நிலத்து	244
ஈண்டு நீர்	109	எம்மை	165
ஈதல் இசையா	181	எய்தி	325
ஈனமாய்	198	எறிநீர்ப்	275
உடாஅதும்	10	எறியென்	363
உடுக்கை	141	என்றென்றும்	160
உடைப்பெருஞ்	368	எனக்குத்தாய்	15
உடையார்	160	எனதென	276
உணர உணரும்	247	என்பாய்	292
உண்டாய	284	என்றும்	306
உண்ணான்	9	என்னானும்	5
உபகாரம்	69	என்னேமற்	330
உயிர்போயார்	50	ஏட்டைப்	358
உருவிற்	239	ஏதிலார்	228
உருவும்	102	ஏமாந்த	378
உலகறியத்	204	ஏற்றகை	98
உளநாள்	324	ஒண்கதிர்	176
உள்கூர்	288	ஒருநன்றி	357
உள்ளத்தால்	128	ஒருநீர்ப்	226
உள்ளத்துணர்	386	ஒருபுடை	148
உள்ளம்	380	ஒருவர்	308
உறக்கும்	37	ஒக்கிய	129

பாட்டு	பாடல் எண்	பாட்டு	பாடல் எண்
ஓதியும்	270	கல்லோங்குயர்	283
ஓலைக்	397	கல்வி	135
கடகம்	289	கழிந்தார்	49
கடக்கருங்	398	கழுநீருள்	217
கடமா	300	களர்நிலத்து	133
கடித்து	156	கள்ளார்	157
கடல்சார்ந்தும்	242	கற்றதூஉம்	314
கடிப்பிடு	100	கற்றறிந்த	256
கடியெனச்	364	கற்றனவும்	340
கடுக்கி	189	கற்றார்	260
கடுக்கெனச்	348	கணைகடல்	138
கடையாயார்	216	கன்னனி	334
கடையெலாம்	297	காணின்	84
கட்கினியாள்	364	காதலார்	73
கணங்கொண்டு	25	காலாடு	113
கணமலை	353	காவா	63
கண்கயல்	395	காழாய	342
கண்மூன்று	400	குஞ்சி	131
கப்பி	341	குடநீரட்	382
கம்மஞ்செய்	393	குடரும்	46
கரவாத	304	குலம்	333
கருங்கொள்ளும்	387	குற்றமும்	230
கருத்துணர்ந்து	211	கூர்த்துநாய்	70
கருமமும்	250	கேளாதே	30
கரும வரிசை	249	கொடியவை	368
கரும்பாட்டிக்	35	கொடுத்தாலும்	274
கல்லாக்கழிப்பர்	366	கொய்புல்	350
கல்லாது நீண்ட	250	கொலைஞர்	331
கல்லாது போகிய	169	கொல்லை	128
கல்லாமை	145	கொன்னே	55
கல்லாரே	139	கோடேந்	354
கல்லெறி	66	கோட்டுப்பூப்	215
கல்லென்று	253	கோதை	71

பாட்டு	பாடல் எண்	பாட்டு	பாடல் எண்
கோளாற்றக்	191	தாம்செய்	120
சக்கரச்	346	தாமேயும்	327
சான்றாண்மை	142	தாழாத்	14
சான்றோர்	126	தான்கெடினும்	80
சிதலை	197	திருத்தன்னை	309
சிறுகாபெருகா	110	திருமதுகை	291
சிறுகாலை	328	தினைத்துணையர்	104
சீரியார்	232	தினையனைத்தே	344
செந்நெல்லால்	367	தீங்கரும்	199
செம்மை	85	துகள்நீர்	2
செய்கை	147	துக்கத்துள்	121
செய்யாத	235	துய்த்துக்	273
செல்சுடர்	394	துன்பமே	60
செல்லா	149	துன்பம்	54
செல்வர்யாம்	8	தெண்ணீர்	44
செல்வுழிக்	154	தெரியத்	168
செழும்பெரும்	352	தெளிவிலார்	214
செறிப்பில்	231	தோணி	136
செறுத்தோ	222	தோற்போர்வை	42
சென்றோ சொற்றளர்ந்து	24	தோற்றஞ்சால்	7
சொற்றாற்றுக்	13	நச்சியார்க்	299
தக்கவாரும்	313	நடுக்குற்றுத்	93
தக்கோலம்	43	நடுவூருள்	96
தங்கள்	337	நட்டார்க்கும்	271
தண்டாச்	62	நட்புநார்	12
தமர் என்று	229	நம்மாலே	301
தம்மமர்	392	நயவார்கண்	267
தம்மையிகழ்ந்தமை	58	நரம்பெழுந்து	153
தம்மையிகழ்வாரைத்	117	நரைவரும்	11
தலையே	365	நல்லகுலமென்று	195
தவலரும்	137	நல்லார்	298
தளிர்மேலே	355	நல்லவைசெய்	144
தனதாகத்	278	நல்லவைநாடொறும்	338

பாட்டு	பாடல் எண்	பாட்டு	பாடல் எண்
நல்லார் எனத்	221	பல்லார்	156
நல்லார்நய	265	பல்லாவுள்	171
நல்லாவின்	115	பல்லான்ற	152
நளிகடல்நல்	243	ஊரங்கண	175
நளிகடல் நாள்	166	பழமைகந்தாகப்	380
நறுமலர்த்	209	பழையர்	419
நன்னிலைக்கண்	248	பனிபடு	87
நாப்பாடம்	312	பன்றிக்	257
நாய்க்கால்	218	பாடமே	316
நார்த்தொடுத்	26	பாம்பிற்	375
நாலாறும்	383	பாலால்	258
நாள்வாய்ப்	207	பாலோடளாய	177
நாறாத்	266	பாவமும்	295
நிலநலத்தால்	179	பிறந்த	285
நிலையாமை	52	பிறர்மறை	158
நின்றன	4	புக்கவிடத்	83
நீரினும்	282	புணர்கடல்	264
நீருள் பிறந்த	359	புதுப்புனலும்	370
நீர்மையை	289	புல்லாழுத்தின்	155
நுண்ணுணர்வினா	233	புல்லாப்புன்	255
நுண்ணுணர்வின்மை	321	புறத்துத் தன்	307
நெடுங்காலம்	138	புன்னுளி மேல்	29
நெருப்பழல்	194	பெயர்பால்	97
நேரல்லார்	142	பெரியர்	125
நேர்த்து	134	பெரியார் பெருநட்புக்	77
பகைவர்	311	பெரியார் பெருமை	170
படுமழை	97	பெருகுவது	234
பண்டம்	118	பெருங்கடல்	332
பரவ	158	பெருநடை	343
பாடமே ஓதி	316	பெருமுத்	200
பருவம்	88	பெருவரை	186
பலநாளும்	284	பெறுவது	317
பலநாளும் சென்ற	229	பெறுவதொன்	335

பாட்டு	பாடல் எண்	பாட்டு	பாடல் எண்
பொத்தகமே	318	முற்றுற்று மடிதிரை	90
பொத்தநூற்	376	முன்னரே மதித்திறப்	92
பொழிந்தினது	259	மூப்புமேல் மரீஇப்	326
பொழிப்பகலம்	319	மெய்ஞானக்	311
பொறுப்பரென்	161	மெய்வாய்கண்	59
பொற்கலத்துப்	206	மெல்லிய	188
பொற்கலத்தூட்டிப்	345	மைதீர்	347
பொன்னிறச்	269	யாஅர் உலகத்	119
பொன்னே	162	யாஅர் ஒருவர்	127
மக்களால்	38	யாக்கையை	28
மடிதிரை	224	யாமாயின்	293
மதித்திறப்	61	யானை அனையவர்	213
மரீஇப்	220	யானையெருத்தம்	3
மலைநலம்	356	வடுவிலா	114
மலைமிசைத்	21	வயாவும்	201
மல்குதிரைய	263	வலைவைகள்	268
மல்லன்மா	296	வழங்காத	277
மழைதிளைக்கும்	361	வழுக்கெனைத்தும்	162
மறுமைக்கு	183	வளம்பட	107
மறுமையும்	95	வற்றிமற்	78
மற்றறிவாம்	19	வாழ்நாட்	22
மனத்தால்	170	விரிநிற	164
மனைப்பாசம்	130	விருப்பிலார்	210
மன்றம்	23	விழைந்தொருவர்	339
மன்னர் திருவும்	167	விளக்குப்	52
மாக்கேழ்	41	விளக்கொளியும்	371
மாண்ட	56	வினைப்பயன்	33
மாற்றாராற்	67	வெறியயர்	16
மான அருங்கலம்	40	வெறுமை	329
முட்டிகை	208	வென்றிப்	315
முட்டுற்ற	240	வேம்பின்	245
முயங்காக்கால்	391	வேற்றுமை	75
முலைக்கண்ணும்	391	வைகலும்	39
முல்லை	45	வைப்புழிக்	134
முற்றல் மக்களால்	237		